D1038250

Crossing Wildcat Ridge

PHILIP LEE WILLIAMS

Crossing

The University of Georgia Press   *Athens and London*

Wildcat Ridge

A Memoir of Nature and Healing

Published by the University of Georgia Press
Athens, Georgia 30602
© 1999 by Philip Lee Williams
All rights reserved
Designed by Sandra Strother Hudson
Set in 10.5/14 Cycles with Arepo display
by G&S Typesetters
Printed and bound by Maple-Vail
The paper in this book meets the guidelines for
permanence and durability of the Committee on
Production Guidelines for Book Longevity of the
Council on Library Resources.

Printed in the United States of America
03 02 01 00 99   C 5 4 3 2 1

Library of Congress Cataloging in Publication Data
Williams, Philip Lee
Crossing wildcat ridge : a memoir of nature and healing /
Philip Lee Williams.
    p.   cm.
ISBN 0-8203-2090-0 (alk. paper)
1. Williams, Philip Lee—Health.   2. Heart—Surgery—
Patients—Georgia—Biography.   3. Wildlife watch-
ing—Georgia.   I. Title.
RD598.W494   1999
362.1'97412'0092—dc21
[B]   98-33579

British Library Cataloging in Publication Data available

Photographs of Wildcat Ridge by Philip Lee Williams

As always,

for

LINDA

Acknowledgments

I would like to express my deepest thanks to several individuals important in the writing of *Crossing Wildcat Ridge*. For reading and commenting on the medical sections of the manuscript, I am grateful to my cardiologist Dr. Daniel H. Magill III and my cardiovascular surgeon Dr. Vincent Maffei, of Athens, Georgia. In addition to helping with this book, they saved my life, and my gratitude to them is boundless.

The anonymous reviewer for the University of Georgia Press was especially helpful in comments on the nature sections of the book. My editor, Karen Orchard, gave me sound advice in cutting what was originally a much longer manuscript. Charles East helped greatly with suggestions for tightening and re-arranging. Some versions of the nature sections in this book began as commentaries I presented on WUGA-FM, the National Public Radio affiliate, also in Athens. Any mistakes in this book, however, are mine alone.

In addition, I would like to thank my friends and family who helped bring me through a very dark time in my life. Bless you all.

Preface

Crossing Wildcat Ridge involves a counterpoint between two stories. One deals with the natural world of the area where I live with my family in Oconee County, Georgia, and the other is about open-heart surgery that I underwent in February of 1994. It is my hope that one story illuminates the other. The story of my surgery is chronological, beginning with the discovery of a heart disorder when I was in my late twenties. The nature sections are arranged by season, but within those sections I write about events that happened at different times during the past seven years. Thus, right after the section describing my return from the hospital in March, we find ourselves in a nature section about winter. I hope readers will not be confused by this arrangement.

Prelude

Wildcat Ridge

I am a country man, raised in the fields and woods of north-central Georgia. I do not care for cities, and so I live in the forest on a ridge over Wildcat Creek, a bold stream that flows, half a mile away, into the Oconee River. The ridge has a reputation for its rattlesnakes, but I've never seen one. There's a dirt road across the creek called Wildcat Ridge, but I think of all the high land along the creek by that name.

Our house is halfway down the ridge, just before it plummets sharply to the creek. I have found archaic chert scrapers on our property, more recent potsherds with intricate decorations. I say that we own these seven acres, but we're really just passing through.

*

It's midsummer today, the solstice. Rain falls pleasantly. When storms come, the forest seems to hiss, and Wildcat Creek changes. I have cut paths down to the creek, and I take Megan, my daughter, to splash and walk there. The sandbars change, pottery washes up, driftwood is beached. I understand that the creek is not a metaphor, means nothing, but I impress meaning upon it. The changes in course, the bank undercuttings mean this or that.

I take as much comfort sometimes in belief as I do in knowledge.

*

In July the blackberries come into bloom. My brother Mark teaches anthropology at the University of Georgia, and he once asked a class if they'd ever picked wild blackberries in the summer. The students looked at each other. They hadn't.

I grew up scouting the blackberry patches, picking a hatful, and then eating them until my face was smeared blue-black and

3

I was drowsy in the pine shade. I take Megan walking on the dirt road where we live, and we check out the blackberries to see if they are ripe. She doesn't care for them, but she pretends to because I love them so much.

The last time we went up there and walked along the road at the ridge crest, we saw a tom turkey and his hen, along with their twelve young. The adults waddled off into the woods, and the babies curled up in line and followed them single file, like a marching band executing an elaborate maneuver.

*

Wildcat Creek is on Civil War–era maps. This part of Oconee County was very secluded until several years ago, when the county paved Oliver Bridge Road, the main route out here. Now they've paved just about everything except *our* road, which is a private lane for us and maybe five other families who have turned away from neighborhoods. We live apart from each other, speak rarely, live quietly.

Wildcat Creek is strong and lovely, and in the winter you can see it from our back deck. Come summer, the white oaks fill out, the underbrush of polk and wildflowers, other greenery. Our house is at the edge of what was once farmland, and down in the woods you can still find strands of rusted barbed wire woven into the trees, which have grown over the barbs, healed the wounds, and spread their canopies.

The creek in flood is awesome, a sudden reminder that even the stones and the native azaleas have no sinecure.

*

Red-tailed hawks nest here, and in the winter a vast flock of flapping turkey vultures overwinters for several weeks. Sometimes, high in the sky over what was once pastureland half a mile away, small, indistinct birds high up harry the red-tails, refusing to let up, to back away.

There is a kind of sublime indifference to process in the forest. Some animals are faithless lovers, others mate for life.

*

We have fire ants. My neighbor goes around sprinkling white powder on the mounds, but we ignore them as we can. Stories about the ants killing livestock seem to be untrue. I ran over a small mound with my lawn mower, and the workers had the mound rebuilt in less than an hour. I am envious of that prodigious and instinctive energy. There is no uncertainty in that world; each knows his job, doesn't know why, can't ask. None knows he will die.

*

The blue jays were shrieking, and my wife Linda said, "Is there a snake out there?"

I went out on the porch at dusk, and the birds were harrying an enormous owl that flew defensively from one pine limb to another. More than two feet tall sitting, with a wingspread approaching three feet, the owl sat and ducked, then flew off, the shrieking jays following him into the dark forest.

Blue jays have an unfortunate song, but they are the sentinels of the avian world and warn of intruders. The owl was mature, hungry, a predator. They are difficult to see because they become active only after dark, though we can hear them.

It is odd to me that we see so little of the world at work. Well more than half of the photosynthesis on earth is done by algae, for instance, but no one has ever raised a celebratory pyre to algae.

*

It's easy to see which part of the ridge was used for farming. Everything that was in cultivation for many years is covered in pines, the first succession in this part of the South. At the ridge-break, where it suddenly plummets to the creek, there are only hardwoods—the climax forest. At the water's edge there are enormous beech trees with their leaves that turn toasty-golden in the fall. They have smooth, even bark that invites the biological graffiti of visitors. Years after a name is carved, the bark breaks out in a pattern of healing, and the words begin to fuzz and fade.

I try to imagine the pine slope bare and rutted with plowline and cotton plants, but my imagination fails me. In the time marked by geology, the agriculture carried on here for two centuries is less than an eye-blink. There are people who remember when this land was used for farming, but no one seeks them out to ask about it. That cultural memory will fade. The remains of barbed wire in the forest will fall away and leave only the forensic bulge of scarred trees.

*

Bats hang close to our house, get inside sometimes. One came into our son Brandon's room one spring night, and as a quiet and tenderhearted young man he captured it and took it outside in a shoe box. The bat, too overwhelmed to come out, had to be coaxed, and in the process it bit through the glove Brandon wore. So: rabies shots, gamma globulin shots, a tetanus shot. He bore it well, not complaining or wishing he had not rescued the wayward bat. Doctors give rabies shots in the arm now, not in the stomach as they did years ago. The gamma globulin shots go in the hip and make you terribly sore.

Creatures out here are curious about the house, an anomaly in their world, and they come to the porch or inside as they think to. A wayward mouse does not get far in here because we have three house cats, one of whom is a frustrated Great Hunter. It's hard now to feel benign about even a mouse because we know they harbor hantaviruses.

The creatures and plants around us do not kill or poison us by design for the most part. Salmonella is looking for a host, not a victim. The bats are seeking out shelter for their sleep. They need protection as they sleep hanging from their feet with their wings wrapped around them like clerical robes.

*

Our porches crawl with anoles, tiny green lizards that vigorously display a red wedge of skin beneath their throats while performing push-ups in the sunshine. From their behavior, I suspect it is more to threaten intruders than to attract mates.

Our cats do the same thing: an autonomic response of fluffing up in the presence of danger or fright. They appear larger, signal their willingness to engage. I am less autonomic as the years unwind, more prone to hesitate, to dodge. I do not know at what age the anole is middle-aged or what threats it must face after its days of territory and mating have passed.

*

Last night I walked to the creek and scared off a large doe drinking the clear running water. She bounded away, across the stones and into the flat marshy floodplain beneath the heavy shade of elms and oaks.

Her hoofprints were deep and fresh in the mid-creek sandbar, already filling with water, losing their shape. I often find the tracks of deer, raccoon, turkey, and wandering dogs. After rain or a few days' exposure, the tracks begin to shift their shape, as if made by creatures who do not exist.

My tracks do the same thing. They fill in. The concave shape of my hard bare feet becomes soft and light, as if a boy had run in the sand and disappeared down the water line.

*

A yellow-orange shelf fungus has taken over the forest floor. I tracked it from the creek up the sharply rising hill, a distinctive smudge that is spread like butter on a biscuit. I lay on my stomach and tried to smell it, but its odor is that of the forest, muted and loamy, indistinct and offering nothing of itself to a hungry mammal. The pulpy heads of the mushrooms are irregular, like a metastasizing cancer, but somehow calming. Fungi can spread for yards, part of a single enormous organism that sometimes pops up to try the air and water.

I have looked for the poison ones and haven't found any, but

I suspect my taxonomic skills are weak. The pulpy yellow petals stop short of my yard, where the conditions for their growth are obviously poor.

*

I have been feeling wayward lately, as if I were planning a trip without a destination. Why do we feel we have to journey to see a new world? All my life I have been a mental traveller, though I have been few places.

A friend told me of her sister's wedding that took place in Atlanta over the weekend. Her grandfather came—the first time he'd ever left the state of North Carolina. I had an aunt who never saw the ocean. And yet I feel as if I know nothing whatever of this ridge, these woods, or the creek. I lack nomenclature. I believe that when I walk away from the house I am going *to* and will return *from*, but I shrink from such terms. At any moment, there is only one direction, one presence, one line of sight.

I pushed over a dead tree last night and immediately worried I had destroyed a habitat. When things are ready to fall, they will. When creeks are ready to rise, they must.

I suspect I am old enough to know there are no directions, no fate or agonies of life that we feel: they are our impositions on the world, our time when we must move, because one day that motion will stop.

*

I think about bark. You can pull it off in shingles from the white oaks and can scrape it (with difficulty) from beech. Pine surrenders easily and is prone to beetles that bore beneath that armor and begin the process of degradation. Bark protects only selectively. Millennia of learning to be a genial host have given it a symbiotic role, straining out most insects who will harm the tree and letting in those who make their homes, reproduce, and die but do not bore too deeply to kill.

When trees die, they shed their bark. When I see piles of bark at the foot of a tree and the leaves browning or gone, I know that soon pileated woodpeckers will be knocking holes in the softening wood. I like that process of becoming useful to others as you age and die. The closer a tree comes to death, the more insects, birds, snakes, fungi, lichens, and such make it their home. It is comforting to think that when the tree lies down in the forest to rot away, it is among friends.

*

Brandon has cut the grass, and it smells wonderful. I am curious: Why has evolution led us to enjoy the aroma of mown grass? Why do certain compounds smell so foul to us? If the latter is to warn us away, is the former to attract us? Does that mean we may have originated as grass eaters instead of omnivores?

Our canine teeth argue against the theory. Science is the art of doubt. The time we have *not* believed in spontaneous generation is a finger snap. I am always amazed that people do not understand the difference between the factual and the speculative.

Most of life to me is speculative, from the purpose of aroma to the muscles of the heart. Our books argue that we know much. Our history as a species argues that we know nothing at all, and remember little of what we have been taught. We learn best the lessons that have moral lessons attached, the kind that bear warnings.

*

There is evidence on Wildcat Ridge of things unseen.

I have not yet seen a raccoon, but their sharp-toed tracks make a highway to the creek. I often hear the hoot of a woodpecker but cannot find the bird with multiple scannings of the limbs. In winter, mice clatter about in the walls of our house, keeping warm and speaking to each other. I find pottery but I cannot adequately imagine the Indian woman who made these cooking vessels.

And yet I believe them. I believe that what I cannot see can exist, just as I know the birds that have not seen me recognize my presence. I know there are raccoons because of their tracks.

I have asked God to leave tracks in the mud, but I have seen none, unless God is a small forest-dweller who washes his food. I try to recapture innocence, but it eludes me, though it does not mock me and it does not condescend.

*

A fat spider outside the window of my study hangs by a strand, having taken in her web for the night. I assume she has fed. The breeze makes her tremble, dangling like a trapeze artist.

Now the art begins once more, the symmetry of spun silk. A fly caught in that web struggles to death, but I find it elegant and purposeful. We can watch that act with little passion and great interest, but we cannot see the weak deer hunted down by feral dogs with anything but disgust. We react to the death of Mammalia so differently from that of other classes. Even belonging to Chordata does not make us familiar. The distance from kingdom to species is the distance from curiosity to fright.

The little spider with the plump abdomen does not frighten me.

*

Natural selection is amoral and lovely. Those who are weak, who have genes that can weaken future generations, are weeded out. Nature is in the business of eugenics, and we can do nothing about it in the long run. A gene for albinism will ensure that wild creatures who are born white will be easy prey (unless they have selected for it, like polar bears or snow hares). A trait for dwarfism in a plant may leave it in better reach of animals who graze. Thus: the line dies.

I spent fifteen years as a newspaper editor before my first novel was published in 1984. In 1985 I came to the University of Georgia as a science writer, and since then I have published seven more novels. I suppose I have evolved, but I never thought I would succumb to an early illness, much less serious depression.

I love the picture that has come down to us of Gregor Mendel, the determined and endlessly curious monk, making crossings in his garden. We have carried that further, and now we can discover the genetic traits that kill us early, may even be able to correct them in adults.

I look in the mirror and see, in that light, a man who should be dead and buried.

A Natural World

Barlow's Syndrome

In my family history there is great creativity and energy, musical talent, high humor, a love of science, and a bent toward poetry by a low winter fire. There is also emotional instability and heart disease.

The good massively outweighs the latter, and I have had a life filled with multiple joys and happiness. I had a pastoral and dreamy childhood and spent my waking hours in the fields and woods, exploring and pretending to virtues and courage I would not develop in later life. I remember frontal assaults on German positions, artillery duels with Union soldiers, sword fights with pirates. And I remember the silence and the solitude. I would spend hours alone in the woods listening to birds and looking for interesting rocks. And I would hear the tales of my family, none of which was within a hundred miles of our home in Georgia where my father was a high school chemistry and physics teacher.

My father's father died in 1935, fifteen years before my birth, when Daddy was only twelve years old. It was his heart. He was forty-three years old. My father's brother, Vincent Astor Williams, known to all as Sambo, came to believe because of their father's death that he, too, would die at forty-three. Early on the morning of his forty-third birthday, entering into the terror he had predicted for himself, he died of a heart attack. I was eight years old. I looked into his coffin. He was the first dead man I ever saw.

As a boy, I brooded over those deaths, over the fact that both of my father's parents died before I was born. Arthur Samuel Williams was a shoe repairman with a shop in a little street called Ramcat Alley in Seneca, South Carolina. He was one of three brothers who married three sisters. His wife (and my grandmother) was Isabel Jaynes. She died of stomach cancer in 1947.

My grandfather's early death had a profound effect on my life. My father, at that important stage of life, was thereafter raised by his mother and a maiden aunt, Elmira Luis Williams, called "Aunt Ellie."

*

I cannot find reason in the paradox of sudden loss and sudden freedom. My grandfather was a quiet man, and his pictures show a lean face, careworn and serious. And yet he was a fiddler who played, with a group of friends, what was called "mountain music" in the twenties and thirties. We now call it bluegrass. He appreciated the arts, though he also loved fox-hunting. He was of normal height, had false teeth, and his nephews, for reasons I have never been able to find out, called him Uncle Auk.

After he died, my father became more introspective, more inclined to the arts of music, writing, and science.

*

It's the spring of 1976, and I decide I should have a physical exam. I am particularly worried about my heart, given what I believe to be a family history of cardiovascular disorders. I am in the newspaper business in Madison, Georgia, a young associate editor, married for four years and rising in the profession.

I assume I will get a clean bill of health. It will help put behind me the phantoms of two dead men. I pick a young internist in Madison named Rose Ann Weaver. Dr. Weaver is pushing the concept of "wellness," and so she applauds a young man coming in to get the first of what promised to be annual exams. I am jocular, effusive even, mentioning nothing of my worries. It will take an hour, and I'll be back at work.

She does all the usual tests, listens to my lungs and heart, hears nothing out of normal ranges. I joke with her, talk about a novel I am beginning to write—a sublimely bad effort from which I learn a great deal. Last is the electrocardiogram. She hooks up all the patches and stands by the machine waiting for the tape to read out. I am grinning and breathing evenly, as if I can affect it, polygraph style.

"Hmmm," she says. "We might need to do this again."

*

And so she does. The second time, the results are even clearer. She doesn't say that it is all right, doesn't act alarmed either, just perplexed. The room seems profoundly silent, something unopened from the Valley of the Kings. I struggle to keep my brain from racing ahead, but there is no disguising the look on her face. She is disappointed.

"I'm really not sure what this is," she says, showing me the tracing. "Your T-waves here are inverted."

She shows me the blips, as if I might understand. I have never heard of a T-wave and try to imagine a context like that of a seismograph.

"They're inverted?"

"Yeah, they're supposed to go this way, and they're—well, you can see."

I feel a ghastly plummeting sensation. My mouth goes dry, and I wait for her to tell me what to do. The answer is to wait a few days and do it again. Perhaps it is an anomaly.

*

I cannot concentrate. I sit and stare when I get home, become a creature of movement without purpose. I take long walks, and they don't help. I feel as if I might go mad. Dr. Weaver does another EKG, and it shows even clearer that my T-waves are inverted—perfectly so. She is stumped.

"Maybe we might, uh, send you up to Emory," she says. Emory: a major university hospital in Atlanta, sixty miles away.

"Okay," I say.

I walk out of her office in a state of collapse. I resent the world, hate my fate, blame myself, try without success to raise a mental insurrection against those T-waves. I may change them by a simple act of will. When I arrive at the office, I tell the editor that I am losing my mind. I walk out the door and don't come back for three weeks.

*

I take no pride now, more than two decades later, in revealing this. Then, I saw it all on a microscopic scale, one man in decline. To me it was my life only, with no meaning or context. I could not know how little one understands at twenty-six.

The earth was a mourning place. I would never compose a symphony, write a book. Only I knew what the sentence was. Only I could understand what linked me to one man I never knew and another I saw in his coffin. I would not go gentle into that good night, nor would I rage. I would shudder myself into darkness.

*

We go to Emory, and I am grim, misaligned, unfocused. I spend the day undergoing tests: EKGs, echocardiograms, blood, the works. The technicians speak to each other in the secret language of medicine, and never to me, except to give directions. I feel incidental to the process, to the world.

"We've got prolapse," says one technician during the echocardiogram. I vaguely think this might be something unusual, but I keep my counsel.

After a time they tell me to dress and wait in the hall. My wife and I sit as I listen to the crepe soles of the nurses squeaking along the tile hall floor. I met Linda in 1970 in a biology lab at the University of Georgia. She was looking for someone to dissect her rat and frog and happened to sit next to me. She had grown up in Boston, moved to Atlanta for a couple of years, then went to New Jersey, where she graduated from high school. The eldest of five children, she majored in English at Georgia. We managed to pass the biology course, and I ran into her the following fall, and we began to date, finally marrying in the autumn of 1972. We would go on to celebrate our silver wedding anniversary in 1997 and make a good life for ourselves.

"Mr. Williams?" A graying doctor holding a clipboard calls me into his office—the diagnostician. He wears gray slacks, a white shirt, dark tie, oxblood penny loafers. "You can come in now."

I go in to receive the sentence, oddly elated at having gone through with the tests. We sit in leather chairs, and he goes behind his desk. "It's nothing serious," he says.

"Nothing that can't be fixed," I say nervously.

"There's nothing *to* fix," he says. "What you have is called Barlow's Syndrome or mitral valve prolapse."

He then goes into a lengthy discussion of the heart, discussing valves and their function. One of those precious flaps in my heart, the mitral valve, doesn't close properly and allows blood back into the heart after it is supposed to have been pumped back out. It isn't serious. In fact, there is growing evidence that hundreds of thousands, if not millions of people, have the disorder. It is congenital and possibly inherited.

"What will I have to do?" I ask.

"Nothing," he says, surprised. "You do nothing."

Summer

A wet wind rises on Wildcat Ridge. At night the owls cry,
sending their husky vowels across the creek as it winds east
toward the river. A pair of mourning doves passes the time in
song. Storms to the north and east cast puffs of pink light in
the limbs of oak and poplar, but the thunder never starts, and
the cicada chatter becomes nearly deafening. A possum with
a pink nose-tip waddles onto the porch looking for anything
to eat. Above him, slung between the porch rail and a post,
is a swaying spiderweb, and its owner rests in the middle,
waiting. Stars are faint through the canopy of trees and
humidity. Fireflies begin to wink, their layers of light strung
beneath the trees and out across the grass. The faint aroma
of honeysuckle drifts across the yard. Distant: dogs. Nearby:
moths by the hundreds huddling around a porch light.

Chasing Time

Wildcat Ridge is a metropolis. It is the citadel of food chains, of ordered transition. Animals have had skeletons for perhaps 590 million years, beginning with the "Cambrian explosion," as scientists call the time when fossils began to appear in profusion. Sometimes I feel that humankind is the least-evolved creature in these woods.

I mark the earth's history by men and women I admire: Linnaeus, Beethoven, Marie Curie, Martin Luther King Jr. I cannot rationally approach the Devonian Era 380 million years ago when fish ruled. They plowed the seas, which were a warm garden of exploding life. By then, life had been around for eons, and skeletons had formed life's outline for some 210 million years. Even the dinosaurs have been extinct for 65 million years. Little wonder that humans, these marvelous and terrible thinking creatures, believe themselves so magnificent. In the scope of the earth's history, we are nothing. Our entire species is no more than a gnat on the tongue of a frog.

And yet we stupidly persist in building ourselves into the history of the earth, often in marvelous ways. I can scarcely imagine a world without the slow movement of Mozart's *Clarinet Concerto* or the golden vision of Rembrandt's *Night Watch*. They are our fossil record and must be kept alive. We are the only species that leaves, on purpose, a record of what we *did* rather than who we *were*.

That feeling of celestial smallness is an adolescent rite of passage. We begin to visit seas, to stare at the sky, to wonder, to fear their inevitable loss. We do not wish to be reminded of the pitiful blink of time between *Australopithecus* and *Homo sapiens*.

*

Our problem is scale. Because we cannot visualize micro-biota, we study the stars. Our obsession is time, because we alone (so far as science understands) know that we will die. There is a poignancy in our efforts to become immortal because we try to manipulate our time.

The anoles on Wildcat Ridge aren't time chasers. They live their short lives by natural imperatives—mating and the gathering of insects for food. They do not live past time or scale. They cannot know me from a deer, a dog, or perhaps a tree.

What does it mean that humans have forty-six chromosomes while goldfish have ninety-four? Or is "meaning" an irrelevant term, as "race" is now becoming? I want to understand these things, but I am a time chaser and I must not choose to limit the efforts of my days. Had I rather read of microbes or listen to Debussy? The latter, no doubt, for I want to believe I can hear in nature what he heard in his mind.

But this natural metropolis does not frighten or overwhelm me. If predators roamed, looking for men to eat, I would feel differently, but the bears are gone, and even feral dogs keep their distance. The creatures who attack me are Davids to my Goliath—mosquitoes, chiggers, fleas, bacteria. They navigate me easily. I am no colossus, just a host. We are long-standing companions. We live with viruses like the common cold, die horribly from Ebola, which may not spread too rapidly because it so virulently destroys its host.

But we are smart enough to know viruses can kill us. We have only learned in the last half century that humans may now be able to destroy this earth—our host—as easily as Ebola destroys blood vessels.

*

We do not reproduce because we fear death. It is simply given to us in the natural order of things. We use our children as evidence of our transit, however—an act I find somehow touching. They are our memory, our bookmarks. We may survive in repeated stories for three or four generations before we begin to fade.

From mountain ranges to cytoskeletons, the evidence of things unseen permeates us; we understand nothing, see nothing, hear nothing. We do not think of cell division or organelles when a woman becomes pregnant. We think of first steps, of eye color. We think of time.

And so I sit by the creek, a speck of this incalculable taxonomy, a stranger in the metropolis. If I did not know the limitations of time and scale, I might be a dutiful worker, serving without question for my short life. Instead, I am condemned to strain against these very natural and profoundly indifferent bonds. I will not escape, but I cannot stop fighting against the certainty of death.

It is my birthright, and I hang in it like a spider in her web — waiting.

Genetic Fortune

Nothing can hide my elation after the visit to Emory. I am free. Ghosts evaporate, medicine retreats. My parents are well and happy here in Madison, and in 1978 Linda and I have a son we name Brandon. On the day we bring him home from the hospital, I carry him around the house in my left arm and read from a book in my right hand.

It's Wordsworth: "Lines Composed a Few Miles Above Tintern Abbey."

> . . . For I have learned
> To look on nature, not as in the hour
> Of thoughtless youth; but hearing oftentimes
> The still, sad music of humanity
> Nor harsh, nor grating, though of ample power
> To chasten and subdue. And I have felt
> A presence that disturbs me with the joy
> Of elevated thoughts; a sense sublime
> Of something far more deeply interfused,
> Whose dwelling is the light of setting suns,
> And the round ocean and the living air,
> And the blue sky, and in the mind of man:
> A motion and a spirit that impels
> All thinking things, all objects of all thought,
> And rolls through all things . . .

I ask Linda what pieces of music she thinks we ought to play for Brandon first, and she thinks a minute and says, "How about one of the *Brandenburg Concertos*?" I am delighted, and I cradle him and play the first concerto. And so we christen him with Bach and Wordsworth.

I look at him in his bassinet and thank the stars for this gift, for my family.

*

In truth, I am genetically fortunate. My parents are both brilliant, work hard, and love the arts. My mother is the opera fanatic in the house, but she also reads incessantly, and when I was a child she sang to me all the time. My father has written poetry and music and designed marvelous electronic equipment. He carried *Palgrave's Golden Treasury* with him all during World War II. As if a gift for his father's early death, he was assigned for two and a half years to an Army Air Corps base near Oxford, where he took organ lessons and soaked up the culture. He took a trip once to the Lake Country and went on a walking tour around a magnificent lake called Derwentwater. A rainstorm came and he knelt and threw his OD raincoat over himself only to find, a few minutes later, a sheep leaning on him, perhaps thinking he was a rock.

My father has lived an unimaginably full life, full of science and art. He has helped people by the dozens for no reasons but a personal altruism. He loves Keats and Wordsworth, but he adores classical music, especially Mozart and Bach. He spent the first half of his career as a high school chemistry teacher and principal, and the second half as an electronics design engineer. I cannot recall a time that science was not around our house, or art for that matter.

He and my mother gave me my passionate love of classical music. From my mother came my sense of humor and a love of grammar. From my father came the creative urge. He has painted portraits and landscapes; written poetry, his autobiography, and numerous archaeological monographs; he designed intricate electronic devices back in the early days of what were then called integrated circuits. He was the co-inventor of an ultrasonic monitoring device that scientists used in studies of animal movement. And all this barely scratches the surface of who he is. Above all, he is a man who believes in God, who is eternally curious, and who bears his family name with a quiet dignity that I will never be able to match. My mother taught me to listen to and love opera. They are magnificent human beings.

Still, there are shadows. My Uncle Sambo's death on his forty-third birthday haunts me. I remember him as an amazing man who always had a cigarette in one hand and a beer in the other. He loved to swear, and he played the piano (everything in A-flat) and the saxophone. I spent a week with Sambo and his wife Mac in the summer of 1957. He let me shoot his .38 pistol and his .22 rifle. We plinked beer cans down by his sandy creek.

There were also people with emotional problems in my ancestry, and I always thought of them with wonder and worry.

*

In 1978 I take a job as managing editor of an alternative weekly called *The Athens Observer*, and in 1979 we move the thirty miles from Madison to Athens. I love the job, and the paper is filled with fantastically talented people. I promise myself never to take my health for granted again, and so I start regular yearly checkups with a personable and talented cardiologist named Dr. Daniel Hamilton Magill III. Ham in the early 1980s still looks like the athlete he was in college, rangy and tall. I go in for a checkup every spring. Every other year I go to Athens General Hospital for an echocardiogram.

In 1985, after seven years at the *Observer*, I take a job I have always wanted: I become a science writer at the University of Georgia. Every day I see the world in a different way as I cover the work of scientists and send the stories out to the media. Linda and I have our second child, Megan, in October 1991.

I spend my seven biblical years at the office of Agricultural Communications, then become senior science writer for the university's Office of Public Information in the fall of 1992. My health is good, and science writing becomes even broader and more intense. One day genetics, the next, microbiology. I study all the time and love it.

By Christmas of 1992 I feel as if my life has settled and that I have escaped the curses of my family. There's only one thing: On January 30, 1993, I will be forty-three years old.

*

I have been feeling tired. Walking up the sharp hill from Wildcat Creek to the house is tough sometimes, and Linda asks me why I'm breathing hard. I tell her I'm just out of shape.

My birthday passes without event, and I feel like thrusting my fist up to the heavens and shaking it. I don't. I stay busy with my family, with my job at the university. I see the release of my seventh published novel. I schedule my yearly physical just before my forty-fourth birthday. I have always thought that if I reach forty-four unscathed the curse will be broken, like an old German fairy tale.

Dr. Magill listens to my heart and can't really hear much different and sends me to the hospital for my standard bi-yearly echocardiogram.

"How have you been?" the technician asks. She and I have done this together before.

"Great," I say. She puts EKG patches all over me and smears my chest with a gel that allows the echocardiogram probe to "see" my heart better. We chat about children and the weather and work. She goes through the procedure methodically, having done it hundreds of times. I look at the monitor and see my heart beating, actually watch the floppy mitral valve closing poorly. I've seen it before.

After a time the technician gets another nurse to come in. "Do you read this like I do?" she asks her colleague. They stare, confer.

The second nurse leaves, and mine sits on the edge of my bed in the cold, dark room. "Is somebody going to call you about

this?" she says. "I mean, talk to you about the results of this?"
I feel a heavy, sinking, freezing feeling.

"I guess Dr. Magill will."

"Okay, then."

*

I walk out confused and a little numb. I don't say anything
to Linda, can't imagine what might be wrong. I walk down to
Wildcat Creek and look at the tracks along the sandbars. I leave
my tracks there, too.

The next week the phone rings at my office one morning.
"Phil, it's Ham Magill."

"Hi, Ham."

"Look here, we seem to have a little problem. According to
the echo, your heart appears to be enlarging. I'd like to schedule you for a heart catheterization at the hospital."

"When?"

"As soon as possible. How about next Friday?" He gives me
a time. He will run a probe into the femoral artery in my leg
and push it up into my heart and release dye. He describes the
procedure. He says he doesn't quite know what's happening. I
take it from the unconcerned tone of his voice that it's serious.

"Okay," I say numbly. I hang up the phone. I feel the room
closing in on me.

The Sounds of Wildcat Ridge

I walk alone today, somber and intense. I have come for a distinct purpose: to listen. Megan and Linda are in the house, and Brandon has gone to visit a friend. I blunder on the paths, not understanding the disruption I inevitably create here. If I step on a puffball, I will serve the natural process through spore dispersal. Chiggers and ticks sense me near, a perfect blood meal. I know I offer myself as their host and breakfast, but I don't really care. Sometimes, before a thunderstorm's penultimate updraft, the birds go silent. You can almost taste that lack of sound. It commands respect. But now the forest is thick with avian conspiracies, with wind noises, distant dogs, insects, amphibians.

I want to understand the connections here. The Second Law of Thermodynamics says that the disorder of an isolated system must increase with time or remain constant. Order will not spontaneously arise. And so I place upon this ridge an order of my own making. I come to write in my memory the orchestral score of crows and wind.

*

I sit on a huge boulder high over Wildcat Creek, on a bed of moss and lichen. In front of me a thick beech tree shudders in the wind, leaves swishing. Crows. A red-tailed hawk. The creek's bubble and magisterial progression below. A jerky dance of squirrels in the deep forest leaves.

The air moves by pressure gradients. Now it is summer, and the American South is in thrall to the Bermuda High—the holy emperor of air masses here. In late spring it ridges back over us in Georgia, keeps weather systems away. The air rises, thunderstorms form. The heat is penetrating and wet. Our ignorance is masked by marvelous tools—radar, satellites, computer simulations—and yet our best guesses at the track of a hurricane are often laughably wrong. People rail against science for its ignorance, not knowing science is not a "science"—it's an art. We had studied the weather for thousands of years before we discovered, early in World War II, a speedy river of air called the jet stream.

I feel sad today, and it's not for my smallness in the system. I exult in humanity's puny efforts to scratch the glass of life. And I do not "rage against the dying of the light," in Dylan Thomas's memorable phrase. I want to achieve a great thing—to be a sound in the woods and to humble myself before the physics of sound waves. But I can't. I want to understand, too. The crows laugh at my stupidity with their guttural calls.

A car goes past out on Oliver Bridge Road, a half mile from here. The car is old, has bad spark plugs and a muffler hole. I may know the man. But I cannot say I know the frog that has just leapt into a backwater pool below me. The sound is delicious, a plunking splash. For a time, the wind ruffles the oaks and beeches, but when it subsides, a miracle occurs: a mockingbird.

My God, what evolutionary pressure could create this? There are bel-canto arias, brief stretches of "electronic" static, repeated triplets rising one whole tone at a time, the dying fall of an alto recorder. (Are birds really related to dinosaurs? I cannot believe that a pterodactyl could sing.) I refuse to breathe or turn for fear the mockingbird will stop.

*

The song finally dies after nearly ten minutes. I am very nearly in tears. I have not expected this performance, strain against believing it was sent for me. It was not. I am a millipede here, a disappearing shadow, a crashing mammal in repose upon a rock. My eyes have been closed for a very long time, but I open them now. The trees shimmer with wind. I hear distant dogs, a cow, a crow, a hawk, a cardinal, a lizard in leaves.

Now I want them all to hear me. I get up from the rock and walk down a narrow, steep path to the creek, my boots breaking limbs, rearranging insects, crushing microbial populations. I whistle stupidly, don't care. I come to the edge of Wildcat Creek and recite poetry, get it all wrong, blunder ahead in a tangle of syllables the crows may admire: *What a piece of work is man.*

*

A femtosecond is a millionth of a billionth of a second. Sound lives and dies, is irrevocably changed in such impossibly short periods. Here on Wildcat Ridge, I know my own auditory limitations. I know that I do not understand time.

I hear nothing.

The Cosmological Script

I am an outpatient at the hospital, but I get a room anyway to await the catheterization. I have read enough to know that sometimes cardiologists find problems so severe the patients are sent straight to surgery. I have had nothing to drink or eat since midnight. It's nine-thirty or so, and already the workers outside are hard at it, adding a new wing on to Athens Regional. Pile drivers. Shouts. The guttural roar of heavy equipment. Those men are healthy, are awaiting nothing more than a break or lunch.

Being sick, as I believe I am, makes me part of a different species. I have seen them all my life, the weak and infirm, the dying, those who face the end of things. You can see in their faces which ones are fighting and which ones have given in. Serious illness is a different country that I find unnavigable. I could be a fifteenth-century explorer in a gale off an unmapped coast. I don't know what is ahead or what they might find.

When the heart enlarges, it loses its ability to pump, working harder and harder and less efficiently all the time. The inevitable result is congestive heart failure. Willie Morris's heartbreaking memoir of the novelist James Jones reveals what the last days of congestive heart failure are like. You lose your breath and your strength as that magnificent engine fails in its ability to circulate the blood.

*

I have brought with me a favorite book, Henri Troyat's biography of Tolstoy. That tortured author lived from the Russian dark ages of the 1830s until 1910, always uncertain of everything in private and certain of all things in public. I am reading about one of his religious fits when a young black man from

"Transportation" comes in with a wheelchair. He will take me to the catheterization lab. I gather my hospital gown around me and climb into the chair, leaving Tolstoy on the bed with his own problems.

"Sorry, I'm late, we been busy today," the orderly says. His voice is light and pleasant.

"You could have waited all day," I say.

"I heard that."

We glide down the hall where men and women toddle about with death grips on their walkers. Many of the people here are country-thin, leathery, careworn. One looks like the pictures I have seen of my grandfather, the one who died at forty-three.

We go down silently in the elevator, and I think this is silly. I could have walked to the cath room, but it's not the way hospitals do things. My life does not flash in front of my eyes, but I consider things undone for a moment. Europe. The Rocky Mountains. My children grown to productive adulthood. The young man pushing me wants to chat, and I try, but it falls flat because I'm empty on the surface, lost very deep down inside.

One corridor and then another, and then a turn into the ante-antechamber of the cath room. I am the only one in it, with nothing to read.

"You do good, now. We'll be back to get you when you're through."

"I can't wait."

"I heard that."

After a while a nurse takes me inside to the next antechamber. On either side there are beds and curtains, like a semiprivate room. (What a misnomer! Semiprivate rooms are unprivate rooms, period.) She gets information from me, stuff I've already given three times at the hospital, but I know it's routine. They don't want to catheterize the wrong man.

We chat. She's pleasant, and as usual I try to let her know I have no fear. In truth, I don't have much fear about the procedure, only a morbid fascination.

"You look awful young for this," she says.

"Thanks," I say.

"Well, things just happen. You know my grandma always told me that, and it's true. Things just happen, and there's no reason for it, and there's nothing you can do about it."

"They do," I say stupidly. "Things just happen."

*

Or do they? Some days I think there is a cosmological script to the world, the fine print behind those admonitions in Ecclesiastes. There is more than "a time to live and a time to die," I think, more explicit directions for our lives' quick transit. Or is the world simply a "wound clock" as some philosophers during the Enlightenment decided? Is it all a matter of process and genetics?

And what if you rewrite the script? Is it a matter of genetics that I am supposed to kick off in my early forties?

I have read many diaries and memories of those in battle, particularly the American Civil War. Men would awake on a certain morning and know that the day of their death had arrived. They would give instructions to friends. Some before the larger battles wrote their names on slips of paper and pinned them to their shirts for identification.

I have known many people who lived with a deadly disease for a long time and then gave up and died almost instantly. How do you know? Or do you? What we know of DNA would not fill the proverbial thimble, but what we see hints of "wonderful things."

Somewhere, the gene for this disorder entered my family tree and may have picked off others one by one. In each generation, there may have been one sacrifice to the gods of mitral valve prolapse. Or maybe I think too damn much.

*

I am considering Tolstoy when they come in to get me. I think about the wire they will insert into my femoral artery. I think about it navigating the length of my body until it arrives in my heart.

I think of a man who died in 1935.

Into the Light

There is no romance in nature. And yet I instinctively recoil from the hunter and the hunted as they edge up the evolutionary ladder. I can dispassionately watch a snake slowly consume a frog, but a lion tearing out a gazelle's throat disturbs me.

Today, though, I have come for the light.

Late this afternoon the sun hangs summer-high, and the air is dense and wet. I will try to see past sunlight and shadow. Light is both wave and particle, and the color of light depends upon its wavelength. We have telescopes and microscopes because scientists have studied the nature of light. And yet I am less interested in optics than in memory and perception. What I recall often seems more real to me than the present moment.

Women and men have worshipped the sun for millennia because they feared the darkness. At night you could be attacked or eaten, you could become lost. Threatening sounds came. No wonder ancient Egyptians worshipped Ra. The sun made plants grow and allowed you to see a threat before it reached you. Likewise, I see how moon cults arose and why a full moon brought celebratory feasts in some cultures.

Less clear are the variants of daylight. Weather, climate, and season all bring subtle—or dramatic—changes to the daylight. My impressions of light are stored away, and I bring them out from time to time like sepia photographs for restoration.

*

I sit beneath a thick-trunked cedar where the shade is heavy. Little grows here in the dense canopy, I can sit with less threat of attack by insects that live on woody plants or creepers. I am dripping wet, but I recall a late autumn afternoon from perhaps my eighth year. A cold front had come through Georgia, and I stood in our side yard looking at the wind-bent trees and the sun just above its horizon. I felt a deep unease, a sense of growth and loss that overwhelmed me but also a touch of the pristine. The earth expanded. It was a message I could not decode, a light whose focal point was me alone.

I was cold. The wind blew back my hair. I felt very small and distant from my family, and yet that light chose me for a story I could not know. I felt alone but not afraid, anointed but not for greatness. In that light I felt only a melancholy certainty that the wind, the sky, the sun, and the blowing high clouds had been laid purposefully before me.

That light is now my companion, and I summon it, though I still do not understand.

*

Fire ants won't nest in the heavy shade. Many of the creatures on Wildcat Ridge refuse the sun with equal evolutionary certainty. Humans are omnivores of the light, will even bake themselves brown and give melanoma a place to hold on to the sun. In plant terms, I'm a moss. I dislike direct sun, despise high summer.

The mottled light around my cedar throne seems simple, but I know it isn't. The filters are dogwoods and sweet gums and several varieties of oak. The light comes through on to Virginia creeper, poison ivy, and dozens of perennials whose names I do not know. The intensity and degree of shadow are different every square foot, and so are the microfauna that reacts to it.

In the taxonomy of this place, I am a nonintrusive, transient mammal, and I mean nothing. My own shadow is blunted by other shades, and a distance of twelve feet from earth-borne insects is a light year. I am less a threat than an opportunity. And yet I have seen ants boil into action around their mound simply from the passing of my shadow.

I can understand what light does, but what does it mean? Anything? The sun is setting and the shadows shift around me, and suddenly the greens are changed, the yellows less buttery, the browns a shade darker.

*

Another memory: Christmas morning, 1959. I was dressed in my new red football uniform and had just place-kicked the ball over a privet hedge. The air was chill, almost too cold. And that light! The sun was barely up, but it threw a magnificent glow on the frosty cattle pasture next to our house. I kicked the ball again off my new tee, and then for a moment I stood in that sharp and precious light. It was a perfection, a kind of eternal stillness and peace. My joy was so potent I felt I might fly into the bare limbs of our pecan trees.

Soon we were on the road, making the long drive to my grandparents' house in South Carolina. I felt the glow of that light in my hands and eyes, an ideal sense of peace.

*

Epiphanies come less often these days. I do not have one beneath this cedar tree. But when I reach out from here, my hand goes from the shadow into the benevolent setting sunlight.

Something slow is happening to me these days, and I do not fear it.

Inside the Living Heart

The angiography room is cold. I am more curious than afraid. Dr. Magill is nowhere to be seen, but a cheerful, largely female crew hustles me in and gets me on the table and begins the preparations. Music plays, but at least it's not Neil Diamond. The nurses are friendly, efficient.

"You look young for this," one says.

"It's a valve," I say. I might be describing a problem with my old Ford truck.

"Oh, we get valves," she says, "but not as much as blockages. We do see valves."

The men and women who have shuttled in and ahead of me are older, look sick and afraid. They have blockages. Some will head into the operating room for bypass surgery in a day or so, and others will be told to wait and take their medicine. They will descend permanently into fear. When will it come? In the middle of the night? At a cafeteria just before dessert?

*

A male nurse shaves a patch high on my right thigh and part of my pubic mound. I feel no violation of my body's privacy. Nothing is private in hospitals and there is no dignity. Good nurses buoy dignity as much as they bring comfort and care, and these women and men try. I don't feel indignant.

They cover me with monitor patches. I'm shivering. The room is filled with electrical equipment. I try to gauge my feelings toward all this, and fear is utterly absent, replaced by a growing fascination with the workings of my body and the procedure we're about. They tell me I'll be able to watch the dye released into my heart on the television monitor, and I try to picture it. The music works: a nonprescription anodyne that took God knows how long to make into surgical practice.

The nurses are checking wires when Dr. Magill comes into the room in surgical scrubs. He asks me how I am, and I say fine. No more conversation. The nurses have given me shots in the leg to diminish the femoral slice, the insertion of the catheter. I instinctively turn and look at the monitor and see, with startling clarity, my own beating heart, floppy valve and all.

"You ready?" Ham asks me.

"Yep."

They warn me not to move. Dr. Magill begins to slide the catheter into my femoral artery. I don't feel a thing. The interior blood vessels have no nerve endings, most of which are on the skin and muscle for obvious evolutionary reasons. It only takes a few moments, and the catheter is inside my living heart.

Complications are rare with this procedure. Less than one-tenth of one percent actually die or suffer a heart attack or stroke during it. In fact, the worst problem with it is an allergic reaction to the "contrast agent" or dye, and that affects less than two percent. Still, I've talked to men who developed such a fear of a catheterization that they vowed never to do it again under any circumstances. I find it utterly fascinating.

There are two parts: releasing a dye to check the viability of my coronary arteries and measuring pressures in the right heart, left heart, and aorta. There are predisposing risk factors for complications, and one of them is valvular disease.

Dr. Magill releases the dye, and I feel a minor warmth in my chest as I watch the monitor and see my coronary arteries suddenly visible.

"Well, there are no blockages, but we didn't expect any," he says after a minute. This comes as a tremendous relief, but in truth I am mesmerized at the sight of my heart, that glorious engine that has kept me alive for so many years.

The real problem, of course, is the valve, so the team measures cardiac output and pressures on either side of the heart. I feel drowsy and comfortable. The music and the expert nurses make me feel as if it's no worse than a teeth cleaning. Suddenly Dr. Magill is removing the catheter, and the team immediately applies pressure to the wound in my leg to keep me from bleeding to death.

They do their job and take me back to the waiting area outside the cath room, where I stay for a while until they believe it is safe to move me back upstairs to my room. The procedure hasn't been much to me, and I am not afraid. I know, for instance, that my coronary arteries are clear. That is wonderful news. Now all I have to worry about is that valve. The same young man comes and gets me. In the elevator he's singing a little. I am filled with hope, but I can't say why.

The Wings of a Hawk

My favorite bird on Wildcat Ridge is the red-tailed hawk, *Buteo jamaicensis*. I am struck dumb at times by its magnificence, by its marvelous scream, *keeeer*. That descending pitch is as common here as the sound of a car in the city.

I have seen specimens two feet tall around here, with their white breasts and rust-colored tails, sitting on a tree limb or a telephone pole, watching for movement in the broom sedge or wheat fields. They nest in the massive pine tree down the ridge from our house, just where the land breaks off into a twenty-foot fall to Wildcat Creek. The nest is enormous, made of sticks and bark and pieces of grass and reeds and set very high in the tree.

I have watched the nesting through binoculars from my back porch. I cannot see into the nest, but I know red-tails have two or three white eggs with brown spots. They breed all over North America.

*

The red-tails don't just fly; they soar.

I have stopped my truck on the side of a country road more than once to watch a red-tail hunt over a fallow field. I am always alert to them sitting on utility wires or poles, and I call out in delight when my family travels.

"Big guy," I say when I see one, pointing.

"Yeah," says Linda, leaning to see it herself.

I am a bird-lover, and I know that hawks eat songbirds, but always the red-tails take my breath away, send me soaring with them on rural adventures. I once seriously thought of having a red-tailed hawk tattooed on my deltoid, but I never did it.

I wish I could spend a year doing nothing but studying and photographing red-tailed hawks. Several years ago a red-tail hung out in a huge cedar tree outside my office window on the University of Georgia campus. The hunting must have been good, because it stayed in the tree for weeks and weeks, swooping off to hunt, then coming back to eat.

My office mate and I named him Nick, photographed him over and over.

*

Hawks and eagles are in the family *Accipitridae* and include more than two hundred and forty species worldwide. On Wildcat Ridge, we have red-tailed hawks, red-shouldered hawks, Cooper's hawks, and American kestrels (formerly the sparrow hawk). We probably have more red-shouldered hawks than anything else, and their piercing *kee-yeeear* is more common than the single scream, *keeeer*, of the red-tails. The red-shoulders eat frogs and snakes, aren't quite as big as the red-tails, and have rusty chests, unlike the mostly white breast feathers the red-tails boast. The tails of red-shoulders aren't as big as the ones on their cousins, either.

I am especially fond of the blue jay–sized American kestrel, which I see up near the open land at the crest of the ridge. They don't like deep woods, preferring fields where they can rely on their expertise as hover-feeders. They are easy to miss as hawks, but get a glimpse of that tearing beak and there's no doubt about it.

*

I was leaving Raleigh one dawn, heading home after part of an author tour, when I came to Jordan Lake. I was listening to National Public Radio drone on about Sri Lanka or something when I began to cross a bridge. Halfway across, I saw a bald eagle, hunting. I shouted aloud, slowed, but it lifted that heavy body up as if it weighed nothing, passed me as I passed it. I turned, looked into the mirrors, but it was irretrievably gone, an image of no more than two seconds.

I had never seen a bald eagle in the wild, and I switched off the radio and rode on the crest of adrenaline and profound pleasure for many miles before I landed again, found myself decidedly earthbound on U.S. 74, heading east.

*

I have seen ospreys near the beach, kites in south Georgia, an occasional sharp-shinned hawk. But some are out of their range here, such as the short-tailed hawk (south Florida only), the Swainson's hawk (the American West), and the white-tailed hawk (southeast Texas).

Office workers in Atlanta have seen peregrine falcons nesting in the high-rises. One species, the gyrfalcon, lives almost exclusively in Canada and breeds in the tundra of northern Canada and Alaska. Whatever the species, the family *Accipitridae* members have sharp talons and hooked bills and are birds of prey.

*

I have long wondered why I am so taken with hawks. They are not the most beautiful birds and hardly the most colorful. Their voice is not a song but a piercing whistle or screech. They do not nest near houses and are somewhat difficult to study for the amateur. And yet what strength and poise!

The first day I laid eyes on this house and knew instantly that I wanted it, I saw a thick-chested red-tail gliding over the nearby fields, flapping only occasionally to prevent a stall. The wing-arc of the red-tails, their stunning vision, their subdued color from above or below, still fascinate me. From below, it is light, like the sky, making it less visible to a mouse. From above, it is brown like the soil, so it can blend. Perhaps I admire that camouflage, but it seems to be far more. The hawks are the kings and queens of the hunt in these parts, and they rule the air over Wildcat Ridge.

I will see hundreds of robins, blue jays, sparrows, and chickadees, but one red-tail is enough to stop me in dumb admiration. Could it be that we humans admire certain other animals, species, or families through our own natural selection? It occurs to me that in our dim past the raptors were guides toward links on the food chain. They were the hunters of the air, and we hunted alongside them on the savannah.

Or perhaps that is amateur speculative folly. No matter. That kingdom of flight is our dream, and each of us is Icarus, wings made of wax.

*

I am in my truck going to town when I see a red-tail, plump as a penguin, sitting on a power line, waiting. I pull off the road not far away, open and close the door as quietly as I can, and get out, walk twenty yards until I am almost directly under him. *Keeeer*, I say, trying to imitate its whistle. *Keeeeer*. The hawk shifts from one foot to the other but doesn't leap up or fly, even look down. He looks out toward the pastures where he makes his living. It is a warm, weepy-gray day, and the herd of Holsteins sits in the gnawed-off grass, chewing cud, marking time.

I am not a part of a hawk's world, not an object of desire or fear. I am a cow, a horse, a man, and I have nothing the red-tail wants. I do not speak his language. A hot wind rises and fluffs his plumage, but he does not loosen his grip on the wire. I walk around him, around him more, and he must hear me, but he does not look.

Suddenly he takes a gymnastic bounce from the wire, spreads his wings, and flies down and low across the pastures, not flapping for a very long time, disappears at the far end of the grazing area, into a stand of pine trees. *Keeeer, keeeer, keeeer*.

Escape Valve

Blood is the pilgrim of the heart. It is pushed out, travels through the body, returns with greetings from the lungs. The action of the heart has been known for centuries, but sick hearts have meant dead owners until very recently.

It has only been in the past twenty-five years that doctors have learned to remove part of the saphenous vein from the leg to create a "bypass" around diseased cardiac arteries, for instance. The first heart transplant surgery was before that—Dr. Christian Barnaard in 1967. Still, doctors' fascination with the working of the heart is nothing new. Raymond Vieussens first described the pathology of a disease called mitral valve stenosis in 1715. In his fascinating book *Pathology of Heart Valve Replacement*, South African doctor and researcher Alan Rose reports that it wasn't until 1882 that a doctor sewed up cardiac wounds in experimental animals. But progress was slow.

"Any surgeon who would attempt an operation on the heart would lose the respect of his colleagues," one British surgeon wrote in 1893.

*

The first actual surgery for mitral valve disease didn't occur until 1908, and that was on a dog, who died. Five years later the first operation on a human cardiac valve took place, and again the patient died. The following year a doctor named Tuffier used his finger to dilate a stenotic aortic valve, and the patient not only lived but apparently prospered.

The first human heart catheterization occurred in 1929, when a German doctor named Forsmann performed the procedure on his own heart. Various other operations were tried over the first five decades of the twentieth century, but most of them brought questionable results. Only in 1949, the year before I was born, did three doctors independently repair stenotic mitral valves successfully.

Still, none of this surgery addresses my problem, which is known as mitral incompetence or regurgitation.

By the mid-fifties a few doctors were using plastic materials such as polyvinyl and Plexiglas or even nylon to create artificial mitral valve leaflets. But these were undertaken with the heart closed, and none was very successful. To repair a defective heart, doctors needed a machine that would allow them to take the heart "off line," repair it, and start it again. Rose says the idea had first been raised as far back as 1812 and that in 1926 two Soviet scientists kept animals alive with a heart-lung machine. In 1952, when I was two years old and the genetic time-bomb for my heart was already ticking away, American researcher John Gibbon perfected the human heart-lung machine, opening the era of what came to be called open-heart surgery.

It was not until August 29, 1956, that the first open-heart surgery for acquired mitral valve disease was performed on a patient at the University of Minnesota by Dr. C. W. Lillehei. The operation was a success. Many mitral valves, however, couldn't be repaired. And so researchers began to experiment with ways to repair valves. At first they used immobile rings to give shrunken mitral valves some support. This worked poorly. Partial replacements of the valve with Dacron leaflets came next.

The idea of replacing the entire valve had been studied in tests on dogs but again didn't work well. In 1958 (the same year my Uncle Sambo died) Lillehei implanted an artificial valve in a fifty-six-year-old woman, and that valve, one of the first in history, worked for an amazing six years.

*

In 1960 the first mitral valve replacement was performed with a caged-ball device called the Starr-Edward prosthesis. New versions and new designs come regularly after that.

In the fleetingly small space of thirty-five years, a new method of saving lives has been pioneered by cardiac surgeons all over the world. Severe valve disease no longer means making plans for a funeral. It no longer means lingering in the twilight for a year or two, as congestive heart failure slowly erodes life.

None of this knowledge has the least effect on the fear of it all. A man who does not fear having his heart cut open would be a fool.

The Dunes of Wildcat Creek

As a boy I loved a Walt Disney nature film called *The Living Desert*. One of my favorite parts was the story of dunes, those shifting waves of sand that are sculpted by wind and time.

We have dunes on Wildcat Ridge, but not of the desert variety. Our dunes are on the floor of broad Wildcat Creek, and they are arranged not by wind but water. I have sat for hours watching them form and change.

"I wonder if you could apply chaos theory to the dunes in freshwater streams?" I asked my brother Mark once.

"Maybe," he said.

That may be the right answer from a scientist (which he is), but it doesn't satisfy an interested amateur (which I am). I want to know how they arise, what affects their peaks and valleys, if unseen currents sculpt them in normal flow, how they shift in flood.

As always, I want to know too much.

*

I am sitting on a large rock looking through the clear moving water at the dunes of Wildcat Creek. I feel a deep calm coming over me, and for a moment I think I may have another epiphany like the one from childhood, but it passes. And yet I have a profound sense of peace here watching the dunes shift, trailing sand grains from one peak to the next.

Seeing the dunes truly requires more than attention. It requires light. Wildcat Creek, most of the time and for most of its length, is bathed in the deep shadows of beech and oak and lacebark elm. Even the water striders can appear ghostly and lost in their Olympic gliding. You can get closer to the water and see more when the sun is high, or you can find a place where sun is direct and undappled. I watch the dunes now in a patch of direct sunlight, which penetrates to the brown sand,

49

making it seem translucent and shimmering. When the earth moves only slightly in its daily spin, the sunlight will recede up the creek bank, but now it is strong, and I can see the rippled surface of water dunes.

The individual dunes (dunelets?) are not very long—no more than two feet. At the edge, the sand swirls off them and is deposited farther downstream. Yet a closer look reveals that all of the sand is moving, faster than tectonic plates but slower than wind. The grains move forward from peaks and valley, from rills and ridges.

*

Sometimes I bring my dog Morgan to the creek, and she loves to lie in the shallow running water, to sip and bathe. She disrupts the dunes, but they instantly heal, flow up in smooth succession and fill in the holes she leaves. Now, there is nothing to disturb the waves of silicon dioxide as they march very slowly downstream, through a culvert that runs beneath Oliver Bridge Road, straight on to the Oconee River.

The dunes seem regular but are formed irregularly by the creek's rising and falling with steady rain or summer thunderstorm. In drought, the dunes are exposed to sun, dry out and up, blow away, are trod by deer and raccoons. Their rippling elegance vanishes. When the rain comes back, new ridges form. The false desert of Wildcat Creek returns.

I have watched the dunes in all four seasons and see no appreciable changes during the seasons. And when we walk in the creek or Morgan does, the damage heals so quickly you'd never know we were there.

*

Now, the sand ebbs and flows, swirls and settles. In imagination I can see a sidewinder whirling up over one ridge, a camel angling, big-footed, down another. I see the delightfully nutty but manically driven T. E. Lawrence heading for Aqaba.

I once measured between the ridge tops and estimated the speed of water flow, but as the dunes shifted I could not focus on a correlation. Like the distances between fire ant mounds, they are simply artifacts of the natural world. I chase them with meaning, and they recede into science.

*

Wildcat Creek is not only a place of sand dunes. It has rocky shoals that shift with flood tides, banks undercut by the swift stream, and flat, muddy bars that fill with bits of driftwood, sand, and animal tracks. A section of dunes may be followed by a bed of water-smooth rocks from the size of a grain to the circumference of my fist.

It is a matter of underlying geology. Huge boulders sit high up over the creek on both sides, rocks bigger than cars, and from them I can see the lordly progression of the stream over dunes and shoals, sandbars, and driftwood coves.

*

Linda is the Queen of Crystals. We often head for the creek, and she will hunt for quartz crystals with the zeal of a nineteenth-century big-game hunter while I do it desultorily. We have found dozens and dozens of crystals in the stream, from opaque, yellowish, ill-formed specimens to near-perfect transparent ones.

There are single crystals and clusters of them, crystals less than one-eighth of an inch high and crystals three inches long. Some are perfectly straight, and others come in angled groups that radiate outward. Linda is indiscriminate. She will search until she finds one. As I have said, she always finds a better specimen than I do, no matter what jewel I uncover.

More often, as she hunts for pottery sherds and crystals, I am distracted by the light or the feeling of wind. And often I sit and stare at the submarine dunes and wonder at their shapes and their course. I have never seen a real desert up close, though I have seen the American Southwest by air. I would like to do that some day, but for now I study what I have before me. I see nature's small sculptures, unseen for the most part, even by dogs who lie among them on a summer's day.

The Diagnosis

It's late morning when the black man rolls me, still prone, back into the room on the surgical floor. He and a nurse lift me and put me on my bed, and then the nurse comes back and puts a heavy sandbag on my right thigh. This is to immobilize my leg. I can't move it for six hours, until the blood has clotted sufficiently so that I won't bleed out from the femoral artery.

"Bleed out" means to lose enough blood to die.

"Don't move this," she says. "If you need something, just buzz for me."

"Okay."

I check back in with Tolstoy, and he's still gambling away his patronage and berating himself for every evil impulse. Get a grip, Leo. I watch a little television, but it's talk shows, brain-dead exhibitionists showing their stupidity, egged on by con-science-dead hosts.

I decide to take a nap, but I can't sleep. The sound of jack-hammers outside is deafening as they keep working on the new wing. The workers are not sick. They will go home and have a beer. They do not know who is inside the hospital or why. They don't care to know.

*

I drift to sleep, awaken, only to remember that something terrible may be wrong with me. Linda will be here after a while, when she can get a substitute and arrive at the hospital from her classroom, but now I am alone in the room.

It has been seventeen years since I went to Emory Clinic with my strange inverted T-waves. I look at the door, constantly ex-pecting Dr. Magill to come striding in. He is the bailiff who will read out my sentence. But nothing happens, and the minutes stretch into hours. I doze off.

*

Nothing. No Dr. Magill, no nurses. I have to urinate worse than I ever have, but I can't stand, so I buzz the nurse and ask for a small plastic urinal. I am embarrassed, but I can't relax my muscles enough to use it while lying down. I feel as if I will explode, and then they won't have to worry about my heart. I make a joke about it.

"Well, I can cath you, but then we'll have to run an IV, and you'll have to spend the night," she says. Oh my God. First, I don't want to spend the night. I have never spent the night in a hospital. Second, the thought of this pretty young woman inserting a catheter into me makes me cringe. It's nothing to her, just a procedure she's probably done a hundred times. It's my dignity, not hers.

"I think I'll just hang on," I say.

"You've got three more hours," she says, smiling. "That's a long time to hold it if you really need to go."

"Yeah," I say. She leaves, and I try to use the damned urinal, but it's a fruitless attempt. All I need is a ruptured bladder. The jackhammers are working away again.

*

There are footsteps, and Linda comes into the room, smiling slightly and looking worried. I wave at her and shrug.

"What did you find out?" she asks.

"Nothing," I say. "Nobody's told me a thing yet."

"How was it?" She means the catheterization. When you've been married as long as we have, you rarely need to be explicit to be understood.

"No big deal," I say honestly. "Kind of interesting. My coronary arteries are clear."

"Good," she says. "You need anything?"

"A bathroom," I say. I explain, and she not only has no sympathy, she finds it hilarious and tries not to smile at my situation, fails. "You're not going to think this is funny if I explode."

"I didn't say anything," she says. Then she laughs at me.

*

We are dawdling, perhaps forty-five minutes later, when Dr. Magill suddenly comes striding into the room, looking like he always does. I stiffen. He has a clipboard. He sits on the edge of the bed. "How you doing?" he asks.

"Good," I say. I don't tell him about my problem.

"No bleeding, then?" he asks. He takes a look at the pressure bandage on my leg and nods. Then he stands back up and walks to a white marker board on the wall at the foot of the bed. He picks up a felt-tipped black marker from the tray.

"No," I say belatedly to the question, which has already settled in its own dust.

"Okay," he says. "Here's what we've got going on here." He draws a heart on the board, steps back, takes a look at it, then shakes his head, erases it and draws it again. For some reason, I find his lack of artistic assurance touching. By now, as he re-draws the heart—to represent *my* heart—I know.

"Okay," I say.

Linda slides her chair close to me at the side of the bed. I feel my heart beating irregularly, not closing properly, squishing around in my chest as if it wants to get out.

"Here's what we've got going on here. Your mitral valve is supposed to be closing here like this." He points and gestures. "But it's barely closing at all anymore. So what this is doing is making your heart work harder, and it's starting to enlarge."

Now I understand the worry in the voice of the echocardiogram technician. I feel an ominous weight, but it's in my memory, not my heart.

"So what we're going to have to do is get this fixed so that you've got complete closure of the valve. We actually have more than one option. We might be able to repair it, but failing that, you'll need an artificial valve there to make this work."

He steps back and looks at his drawing, and then turns to me, casual and smiling, reassuring.

"I've got to have heart surgery?"

"It's just six weeks out of your life," he says softly. "This isn't going to do you in."

*

We talk about the options, and I feel a creeping numbness in the vicinity of my spirit, whatever that it. I feel cold and alone. I have completely settled into the foreign country of serious illness. I know that valve replacement is a last resort. I know that without the operation, I will die. Dr. Magill says I can have the operation done at Emory in Atlanta, and I instantly recoil. Emory is one of the best hospitals in the world for cardiac surgery—but I still associate it with the beginning of my illness. Or I can have it done right here in Athens, by this hospital's new heart surgery team.

"I'll do it here," I say.

"Okay, then," he says. He sits on the edge of the bed and pats me on the shoulder. "Surgeon's name is Vince Maffei. You'll like him. I'll tell him you want it done here, and he'll come in to to see you."

"Sure," I say. After he leaves, Linda leans down to me, still stuck in the bed with a sandbag on my ankle. We both cry.

*

I tell myself a story of courage, but I am not at all sure I believe a word of it. I feel myself sinking, falling, and I watch carefully for something to grasp on the way down.

Night on the Ridge

The universe is expanding, even from a single point like Wildcat Ridge. The astronomer Edwin Hubble discovered this in 1923 with an elegant experiment. He measured the wavelength of light from atoms in a lab and then measured the wavelength of light from distant galaxies. That distant light was "longer" than expected. He concluded this meant that the universe was moving away from us, galaxy by galaxy.

Archibald MacLeish said, "A poem should not mean / but be." Perhaps I should expand that to include cosmology. I can comprehend particle physics, but expanding universes, the Big Bang, and black holes elude analogy. Edwin Hubble was a genius, and I'm a worker ant, myopic but stubborn.

So, to the night.

All summer long the cicadas have been screeching. Their noise is almost deafening and decidedly unpleasant to us human types. Frogs join them. We hear the high-pitched cry of tree frogs, the low thunk of bullfrogs talking near the creek in between sessions of bug hunting. At the creek, beneath the summer beech and oak canopy, the stars are missing. So I walk up the ridge to a field my neighbor owns. She will not mind me stopping there to watch her hill fill up with stars.

*

Stars, like people, burn out and die. Stars live by nuclear fusion, and our own sun uses up some 700 million tons of hydrogen per second in its "reactor." That field of stars above me is a drama of chemical birth and death, like gaseous fire ant mounds coming and going. Our knowledge of the stars has expanded dramatically in the past half century and yet most of us still look at them as a kind of celestial dot-to-dot. We might not know Rigel, but we can find the "belt" of Orion. We can spot the Big Dipper, but where is Saturn?

Stargazing makes some people feel small and insignificant, but I tend to become expansive. Some nights I am poetic, but mostly I play God and rearrange the constellations. I create Mickey Mantle and Roger Maris, the "Twins." No Ursa Major for me. I see the constellation Omar Bradley—helmet, hang-dog look, and all.

In truth, I am out of my league, in the wrong army at night. All my life I have been a morning person, getting up with the chickens. (We do not keep chickens, but Mr. Bloom across our dirt road keeps chickens and sometimes goats. Often his chickens wander over to our side and graze, and I enjoy watching them. Once, I found the chickens peacefully plucking worms not twenty yards from "our" flock of wild turkeys.) Still, the stars attract me. If the universe were a golf game, our deepest space probes would be a muffed sand-trap shot. We know nothing.

Ignorance all but demands speculation. I went through a very brief period in early adolescence when I loved science fiction, but I soon discovered that science itself was far more fun. If I go on imaginary star flights, I am not the Magellan of the voyage. The best trip I never made was with Charles Darwin on the *Beagle*. He and Captain FitzRoy had different jobs, the latter mapping land and the former mapping genetic drift. What I would have given to be with them! But that voyage in a sense burned Darwin up, just as thousands of visible stars above me now are slowly (in human terms) flaming out.

    *

Five billion years from now the sun will start its slow decline as it runs out of hydrogen fuel to consume in its nuclear re-actor. It will become a red giant and kill all life on earth. When it cools, the sun will form a white dwarf, a small dense star with nothing much to do. Five billion years—an inconceivable distance to all of us here. The night sky, here on my neighbor's hill, makes me think of time. Our own lives are impossibly short, but so are the lives of stars. A twenty-pound largemouth bass is a monster. A twenty-pound whale is a fetus.

*

Stargazing may be about the search for fixed points. Our species wants guarantees. We want to believe there will "always" be an earth and a moon. But it just isn't so.

Nor is it likely that we are the only life in a universe with millions of stars and planets. Some moons may even harbor life. We desperately want to believe our species is unique not only on earth but in the universe. Considering war, crime, rage, and everything down to petty thievery, we might be rewarded to be the only species of our kind. But for every serial killer, there are tens of thousands of women and men who grow, work, bear and raise the young, and then die. I think of them when I look at the stars.

*

You know the planets in order from the sun—Mercury, Venus, Earth, Mars, etc. Well, you're wrong. During each of its long "years," Pluto is actually at times *closer* to the sun than Neptune.

There goes certainty.

*

Romeo begged Juliet not to swear her love by the "inconstant moon." What, then? The stars burn up, the planets go dead, the universe is moving on. And we don't even know what "dark matter" is. (It's something between the galaxies.) Cosmologists speak of the "edge of the universe," but is that about space or time? Is there a difference? I'll never get off this earth, probably never even get to the Galapagos. Okay, then. I'll visit the night to make sure these stars still cover Wildcat Ridge. I'll revert and howl. I will sing and look for omens.

The Wait

I like Dr. Vince Maffei instantly. From what I hear, everybody does. He's a young-looking man with a slight Cajun accent, dark hair, and a casual air. His assistant is with him and he is smiling and cheery, too.

Dr. Maffei tells me about the options, about what doctors call "prostheses"—different kinds of artificial valves, if the attempt to repair the valve isn't possible. "Yeah, we'll do what we call an transesophageal echocardiogram once we get you in there, and it will tell us if we can repair it or not," he says. "From the cath, it looks like you might be a candidate for a repair. It's better, usually, because then you won't have to take Coumadin."

I ask what Coumadin is, and he tells me it's usually referred to as a blood thinner, but it's not really a thinner. It actually inhibits the Vitamin K–dependent clotting factors II, VII, IX, and X and prevents clots. I tell him that I'm a professional science writer, and he changes his tone instantly.

"Then you know this stuff," he says. "Okay. If we can't do the repair, we go with a St. Jude valve. This is third generation now, and it's really great. Nobody knows how long it will last, but probably the rest of your life."

I try to hold back my rising panic. I have to urinate so badly I can barely stand the pressure and the pain. It seems less comic now than it did an hour before. I don't want to have a urinary catheter or spend the night. I want out. I want to go down to my creek and think about this.

Dr. Maffei draws some on the marker board, and his artwork is, if anything, worse than Dr. Magill's. It's the artistic equivalent of those squiggles on a prescription pad. He shows me how the St. Jude valve has leaflets that open and close, and how it is held by a Teflon ring that is sewn into the muscle of the heart. He looks at his drawing the way Ham did, angling his head as if it might be the Mona Lisa. He knows it isn't. He shrugs and then turns back to me. His casual air is profoundly calculated (I think) and enormously effective. This man is going to slice my heart open.

"So, when you wanna do this?"

Just like that.

"When can you do it?"

"Oh, prob'ly next week. I think we could do it Friday, couldn't we?" he asks his assistant, who looks at some paper in his clipboard and says yes. I feel like I'm scheduling a tire rotation. "Or Thursday. Prob'ly Friday. We can check that out and get it set up."

"That quick?"

"You need to go ahead and get this done. See, timing's the thing. You don't want to do it before it's necessary, and you don't want to wait too long. If you wait too long, you get a lot more complications. No point in doing it too early. We ought to go ahead and do yours now."

"Then, let's do it," I say.

*

Thirty minutes before they're supposed to release me, the nurses help me stand up, check the bandage, and then discreetly step outside the room. I use the bathroom finally, but not completely, relieving only enough pressure so I don't wind up in emergency surgery. Half an hour later they tell me I can go, and I rush to the bathroom and enjoy the massive relief I have craved all afternoon. When I finish, I feel my heart flip-flopping, as if to say that wasn't the problem. That wasn't the problem at all.

*

Thirty years before, I would have been doomed to the slow, suffocating death of congestive heart failure. Now, I have a chance, but I wonder at the justice of it all, if not the propriety. If my grandfather had not died of this malady—I'm convinced it was this same disorder—my father would not have turned toward music and the arts. Everything would have been different for me.

Will saving my life make everything different for my son or daughter? And was this an inevitable part of my family's history? We walk out the door of Athens Regional into the cold late-afternoon of a February in Georgia.

Spreading the Word

Some days on Wildcat Ridge I want to be a perpetual pilgrim. In the nineteenth century they crossed Russia from one end to another. Qualifications? You had to embrace starvation, suffering, uncured illness, exhaustion, and faith, the last often being the hardest.

No thanks. It's enough to let my mind wander, and besides, wandering in the United States could get you shot. We may be a profane people in all, but property rights remain sacred.

A piece of paper in the Oconee County courthouse affirms that my wife and I "own" 6.87 acres from the ridge-crest down to the creek. So if I cannot roam Imperial Russia, begging scraps of black bread and returning a mystic's blessing, I will walk my own land and wait for visions. What would I reveal to the red-tailed hawks and the turkey hens that would change their minds about monstrous *Homo sapiens*? First, we are not all alike. Second, we know little but act as if we know everything. Third, we are obsessed with our life's transit; we think we can gain time and hoard it against death. Because we fear death, we beg others to repent and save themselves, for in their Fall we see our own.

*

The white oak outside my study window laughs at me. All nature mocks the *philosophe*. The rain means nothing. That helpful soil-born fungus called *mycorhizzae* means nothing. Mockingbird arias mean nothing. And yet I want to interpret them to each other, to be the philosopher, the universal translator. I wish to convene the Colloquia of Shared Concerns and point out how ecosystems arise. I want to point out cooperation and conflict.

The natural world would gather around me and with one voice say, *So? What's your point?*

I have thought about it. I suspect those of us who flee to nature for answers have more megalomania than humility. And yet I don't believe what I see. I have no faith in water, earth, air, and fire. George Gershwin kept smelling burning rubber because he had a brain tumor. What synaptic misfortune could make such a thing happen?

*

The pilgrim has no need of truths, only ardor. Pilgrims throw everything away for a thing they cannot prove or see— for faith. When I was in college in the late 1960s, you could plug into the ether simply by joining the counterculture. The feeling was more than heady; it felt like a conversion. And yet in historical terms it was nothing special. We were pilgrims for a short time, but what little meaning existed soon faded into thousands of agendas. Nostalgia is the pipeline to lost faith, and it always seems sad to me. When Jerry Garcia died, people all over the country grieved, not so much for a heroin addict who essentially killed himself as for themselves and their lost pipeline to faith. It is never pretty when gods disappear.

*

Today there is a message in the air from autumn, even though it is still summer. When the season really begins to change, every plant and animal here will know it before I do. Bob and Herb, the two fat squirrels we feed, must have sensed it in the top of the tulip poplars. What's left of my fescue lawn probably plans a beer party, for fescue hates hot weather, exults in the cool dampness of fall and winter. I want to tell Wildcat Ridge about something it already knows.

I stink at evangelism, though. I am better at the self-delusion of pilgrimage, or worshipping at shrines. At heart, I am a silent man, gregarious only by turns, social only by necessity. We wandering pilgrims need not speak, for our silence may be interpreted as wisdom. The owl on the ridge might watch me closely from forty feet up and see my stillness and silence as a lack of threat, which in the world of raptors may be the same thing as wisdom.

And so today I say to our acres: Reveal yourself. Lean down and whisper secrets that I can spread across the world like seeds. I will be a keeper of the mysteries, the Rosicrucian of the creek, the Talmudic scholar of bark. And the plants and animals say, *Huh*?

*

Faced with such indifference, what is the pilgrim to do? What is his vocation when humankind is removed? Mine has been to teach myself. I want to understand chlorophyll, to make peace with mitochondria. My message is one of abject (though cheerful) ignorance. I want to see how fire ants affect soil tilth, why skinks love flat places. I want to have a clue about taxonomy.

I can hear the shelf fungi: *Oh God, he's back. Somebody tell him about mycology and maybe he'll leave.* I will tell them that all things are as the grass and wither, and they will say: *So what*? I will explain what I know of El Niño, since fungi must live in dampness, and they will laugh at me. Fungi laughing. Yes, I can imagine it, which marks me firmly as a nonscientist. I don't see much romance in nature, but I feel an infinite humor and patience.

So maybe I should drive into Watkinsville and spread the wonderful news of nature, its powerful indifference. I would stand in front of Dub's barbershop and proclaim the word of cicadas and mourning doves and polk bushes. I would speak of ant monasteries and highways beneath tree bark and make up meanings for all of them.

I might raise my voice. I could wave my arms. They would

take me in and give me bread and water—in the Oconee County Jail. They would ship me off to Athens Regional Hospital and give me tests. A young man would ask me questions about my childhood and give me a pill and a paper cup full of water. "Now, tell me about the ants," he would say. "Do they speak to you?"

*

I can almost see deer examining my tracks in the soft, wet sand of the creek bed, wondering if I live on grass or blood.

*

Brandon comes inside and tells us to come look. We go to the front porch just after nine in the evening, expecting to see something new from our spiders. They dangle, snare flies and other small insects, bag them up, hide elegantly. The species on the porch make poor webs when the sun goes down: irregular, sometimes asymmetrical, but deadly and purposeful.

We have a powerful quartz light on the corner of the porch for visitors who may not like the total darkness of the country night, and the spider has built her nest there and waits in the corner, twiddling her mandibles. An unfilled bird feeder is next to it, made of bark. It has a perch, and on the perch facing the light and the web is a small, patient tree frog. He waits for insects lured to the light. If he sees three lurking humans, he doesn't seem to mind. Linda gets the camera and takes his picture, and he does not even flinch at the flash.

*

The tree frog is looking at the web. Insects hum and buzz everywhere for the light, some so small they fly through the poorly strung sticky strings. When one hits, the spider is there in a blink, stinging to paralyze, then packaging.

The tree frog doesn't care what the spider catches. The spider ignores the tree frog. They are both after the same meal, but there is plenty to share. The home we have labored so hard to "own" is just another nook to them, a cranny for hunting, a tree limb, a bush. The porch light is the midnight sun that brings them a harvest.

That world is mine to interpret, but how do they see us? We are great, lumbering beasts who do magnificent and terrifying things.

*

The spider does not need a pilgrim to explain the frog. You cannot tell the unexplainable to the unknowing, but I still wonder what they know, what they care about. There have been strange men in my family who might wander the earth begging for bread and water in exchange for secrets from the wind. I could join them in the haunt of spirits and spread my amateur taxonomies over a patient and vastly amused Wildcat Ridge.

Close to the Bone

I lie in the whisper-quiet darkness of my bedroom and hear the rain. It is cold and falls as straight as harp strings. It is a Sunday afternoon, and I have been reading Daniel Boorstin's book *The Creators*, a marvelous "history of heroes of the imagination." I have read the heavy volume before and spent pleasant hours with Michelangelo and Bach and Beethoven.

The novelist Raymond Andrews was a dear friend for many years until he shot himself one starry November night in the back yard of his home not far from mine. At the memorial service some months after his death, a number of us who had known him spoke briefly about his kind and loving life. One after another, we spoke of his sweet temperament, his fierce devotion to his work, his long journey, as a black man, from the racism of the 1930s when he was a boy to the world of the 1990s.

A young African American woman spoke. She came up to the microphone at the Atlanta Public Library with her head tilted back and a look of supreme confidence on her face. "I don't *do* heroes," she pronounced in what I took to be a cold voice. But no. She was merely distancing herself from the intense love we were expressing for Ray. She went on to say nice things about our friend, but I never forgot her thundering defiance.

I would be lost without heroes. Boorstin says this about Goethe: "[His] profligacy with words and his alertness to record every item of his time suggest his hope to find in the world of facts a refuge from his inner uncertainty." I understand that more clearly than any of the natural processes on Wildcat Ridge.

*

I am afraid.

I have tried to visualize the sawing open of my chest, the stopping of my heart so the surgeon can slice into the thick walls to reach the mitral valve. On that day I will, in classical terms, be a dead man. I realize that my heart will be stopped for only an hour or two, but the image of that death surrounds me, enshrouds me as the rain enshrouds Wildcat Ridge. I feel the dactylic skipping of my heart better, now that I know what is happening. I know the leaflet in the valve is atrophied, has ceased its lifelong job. Its life is over. Had I lived a half century before, I would be on the inevitable slide toward congestive heart failure and an early death.

The rain increases its intensity, slackens, comes harder, falls away. I am beneath the covers with a black cat asleep on my legs. I turn out the small light on the headboard of the bed.

The door opens a crack and Linda comes quietly in to get a book. She likes to read on the couch on lazy Sunday afternoons. "You all right?" she asks. I am lying on my back looking at the rain. There is no question that I will lie. We both know it.

"Sure," I say. "Going to take a nap."

"Okay," she says. She is not a weeper, and she knows we have two children who need us. I will lick my wounds in private.

*

Evolutionary fitness is easy enough to understand. It is far more than "the strong survive." And yet I can only wonder what mechanism of selection was at work in my own life, for I have tried to contribute what I have in the best way I know, and yet that is irrelevant. For some reason lost in my ancestral DNA, I have been picked for winnowing. Nature gave me a minor gift with words, and when I ask now why I am so sick, all I get is a shrug. All along, I have thought myself separate, the *other*, in the elegant term pervasively used to describe outsiders of one kind or another. And yet when it comes to the architecture of the body, I am laughably the same. Shakespeare took sentiment apart (as usual) in *The Second Part of Henry the Fourth*: "By my troth, I care not; a man can die but once; we owe God a death . . . and let it go which way it will, he that dies this year is quit for the next."

*

Self-pity is not a country but a slope. A mild case can be like a gentle hill. In the worst cases, self-pity is a free fall off Everest. It is humiliating but understandable. In the 1930s F. Scott Fitzgerald wrote a series of articles for *Esquire* about his own emotional collapse. When Ernest Hemingway responded by mocking his friend's confessions in "The Snows of Kilimanjaro," Fitzgerald was appalled. He wrote Hemingway, saying that even if he felt the need to bare his sorrows from time to time, that didn't mean he wanted his friends "praying aloud over my corpse."

Neither do I. And yet I feel I can survive only by raising my misfortune to some tragic height, a bird falling dead in mid-flight. I would be the prey, and the predator would be heartvalve disease. But as I lie here, I know it is not only false but ludicrous. One death rarely sways the actuarial tables of the world.

*

I am afraid to sleep because I do not want to awaken and remember. And yet the rain, the dark gray sky, and the purring cat all wrap me up. I know it is not a cocoon, though, for when I awaken I will be no different. I will not be damp with change, nor will I have new wings. I doze off anyway, and when I awaken two hours later I remember instantly that I must have surgery and that a man I hardly know will stop the beating of my heart.

*

I walk into the kitchen where Linda is cooking roast beef and green beans and corn on the cob. A variety of mild exhilaration lifts me when I realize there are five days before the surgery;

it is not imminent. Five days can seem like five months or even years.

"Smells good in here," I say tentatively. I have no appetite. I struggle mightily to control my fear and succeed reasonably well. Megan totters in and grabs my leg.

"You hungry?" Linda asks.

"Sure," I lie. I cannot imagine what she must be thinking. I pick up Megan and hold her against my chest, and I feel both our hearts at the same time, beating in a merry arrhythmia. I pour myself a glass of red wine and sip it, and I feel the pleasant warmth of burgundy spill down my throat. I will not let them see what drives me on this rainy Sunday. I will not let them see how close I have come to the bone.

On Eight Legs

I believe we respond instinctively to spiders. We avoid them, knowing too well the creepy-crawly feeling of arachnid footsteps on the leg or arm or—much worse—neck. We have been taught since childhood that the Black Widow is poisonous. We have learned of the Brown Recluse, which can cause severe illness.

My friend Kenny Walker was out cutting his grass in the back yard when he felt what he assumed was an insect bite. Instead, the spot on his leg assumed an acute histamine reaction and soon the flesh became swollen and necrotic. He wound up in the hospital and was lucky not to lose his leg. Spider bite.

We all learned in high school that spiders are not insects but arachnids, with eight legs, not six. We know they spin webs that range from gummy messes to geometric triumphs, that they live everywhere, from gardens to forests to your kitchen. Megan cries, "Spider!" every time she sees a daddy longlegs, but they aren't even spiders. Telling one species from another is often impossible without a microscope.

*

Tonight I'm the Great Spider Hunter, coming not to kill the family *Lycosidae*, but to praise it. I've seen all kinds of spiders on Wildcat Ridge, from the Black Widow to the Metaphid Jumping Spider. The latter species isn't poisonous but tends to give you a heart attack by leaping across your path—or on you—like Carl Lewis in the long jump.

When we lived in town, our house (which was also alongside a creek) teemed with jumping spiders, but I'm looking for wolves today. The name of the *Lycosidae* comes from the Greek word *lycosa*, meaning wolf. They have three rows of eight eyes, live on the ground, and are night hunters. Some dig burrows, but most don't spin webs. Some live under rocks. According to the Audubon Society *Field Guide to North American Insects and Spiders*, some have no retreat at all. There are more than two hundred species of Wolf Spiders in North America alone. There is a trick to finding Wolf Spiders at night, and I've done it once before, so I'm out hunting, wolflike, *Lycosa gulosa*, the Forest Wolf Spider. I have a flashlight, boots, and a keen eye for snakes. Is there a spider call? If so, I don't know it, but I walk very slowly and deliberately, not trying to crush the night-time kingdoms of insects. Birds mutter about my intrusion. A mourning dove back up the ridge seems suicidally sad—or maybe just lovestruck.

I hear other footsteps down the slope toward the creek, but they are of the small quadruped variety. I used to camp a great deal, and you find out quickly what bipedal footsteps sound like. I walk down my path and then go into the woods for about ten feet and squat down in the leaf litter.

*

For a long time I simply don't do my job. I become mesmerized with the forest and simply listen and inhale the fragrance of this world about which I know laughably little. In our rush to climb another Alp or acquire fame and wealth, we often have no idea of the world where we live. As I travel little, my Alps are stones and my alpacas are spiders and birds. Every square foot of this earth is undiscovered country and too common to see for what it is. And yet we miss the rise and fall of great kingdoms, the glory of birdsong, the chain of nature rising and falling, endlessly re-creating itself in variety and scope. We do not see anything. We are blind and deaf and cannot smell, taste, or touch. And so I linger for a few moments, the light off, feeling myself become a boulder or deadfall.

Curiosity brings me back to myself. No matter how I try to lose my ego, even my identity in these woods, I am an intruder here. I am a man without a passport, but I come anyway, hoping I can salvage more than I destroy.

Now. The flashlight is the tool of choice when hunting for Wolf Spiders in the dark, because their eyes have a silvery reflection that catches the light at once. I begin scumbling the leaf litter, my flashlight down, and I don't see anything but beetles and ants and a few millipedes, startled at the light and my intrusion. Do they think? What could they possibly make of this giant pushing them around? The litter is rich and pungent, and I lift a teeming handful to my nose and inhale it, and I think, how utterly wonderful. We must have come to love that aroma by evolution, though I can't imagine why. It is fecund, lovely, almost addictive.

I set it back down and move off another few feet and shine my light again, see nothing, repeat the movement several times. Finally, as I lift a handful, I see the silver eyes of a Wolf Spider, a half-inch specimen sitting quietly and wondering, no doubt, who in the world I am. I see the eyes, the dark brown thorax. He looks hairy.

These Forest Wolf Spiders live from Georgia to Maine to Utah. Or is this the Thin-legged Wolf Spider or the Rabid Wolf Spider? It's hard to tell, and I'm not here as an arachnid taxonomist. He seems stunned by the light and then slowly walks away, back into the darkness.

*

I have only seen one Black Widow Spider here on Wildcat Ridge, and it was on my back porch, beneath a bench. I believe in preservation of species, but I also believe in the safety of my family, so I dispatched it, careful not to get its venom on my hands. Brandon says he's killed a Brown Recluse around the place, but I have never seen one.

Nothing makes your blood pump like the jumping-spider species, and I've seen many of them. We try to capture every insect that wanders into the house and put it outside. I've caught dozens and dozens of moths and let them go, but the job is far less pleasant with spiders. Megan usually shrieks for me to kill a spider, and sometimes I do. Often, though, I let them wander out of sight, then fade out of mind. I find killing anything unpleasant, unless I know it's poisonous. (I would kill a rattlesnake in a New York minute. I know they have a place in the evolutionary ladder, but they don't have a place on my land.)

One of my favorites is the elegant little Grass Spider, which spins its funnel-shaped web in bushes and buildings. They are yellowish, small, and run like Michael Johnson would if he had eight legs. I've seen many Grass Spiders around my house, and I like the vortex of their webs, enjoy their nervous scurrying. There are many species of them, and they eat the insects that hit the web and fall into the tunnel below.

*

I am also fond of the Black-and-Yellow Argiope, which is a shrub and garden spider. It is a handsome creature and likes the sun. I have had a few in the gardenia bush at the west end of my front porch where the sun is strong in the afternoons. A useful anthropormophization is that they are "shy." In fact, they are scared and careful, certainly useful tools acquired over millennia of evolution. I have tentatively identified other species here, from orb weavers to crab spiders, but I am far less sure of them.

I must admit I am less interested in spiders than I am in webs. I have watched a common Garden Spider build her huge web in less than an hour, a gorgeous and geometrically majestic net that waves in the wind. And I have seen Black Widow nests that seemed like a haphazard mess, with filaments strung everywhere. As I love order, it gives me one less reason to feel charitable toward the Black Widows.

Watching the construction of a spider web is a wonderful way to spend an hour on a summer evening. The spiders don't mind to see a flashlight, because they must know that the light will draw insects. I have seen a spider make death-defying leaps from one porch support to another to anchor a fiber, then leap right back for another try. Sometimes the webs are still there in the morning, hanging low with dew, the spider sitting in the middle, unmoving. But more often, the web and the spider are gone by first light.

*

There are eleven orders of spiders, more than 75,000 species worldwide, and 4,000 in North America. They have been around—get this—for 350 million years. They live in extremely wet climates and deserts. They can be almost microscopic or as fat and hairy as the tarantula. They are both completely benign and very poisonous, though deaths from spider bites are rare.

*

I keep pushing back the leaf litter and find several more Wolf Spiders with their silvery eyes, but then my attention starts wandering, for a screech owl has started his rough song, full blast, not far away. I stand and turn off my light and become an insignificant part of their kingdom.

Nothing fears me there, not spiders or owls, or mourning doves. Nothing minds the sound of my steps as I walk back to the trail—at least the forest sounds do not quieten. My only advantage is size, not speed or cunning. I know I'll probably have ticks on my legs when I get inside, for they know me only as a host.

I imagine silk being spun, great blankets of fine fabric in the night.

Things in Their Order

I am at my desk on Monday, arranging my life. The death rate from valve-replacement surgery is tiny, especially for someone my age, but I have a family. I have obligations to make sure my life is in order. And yet what a strange phrase! Whose life is ever really in order? Our emotions are strong or fragile depending on the day, even the hour. I am somewhat grim but not teary, and so I clean out files, throw away the debris of my professional life as a science writer. My desk begins to take on the order of fanaticism.

A woman at the office sticks her head in the door and looks around at my half of the room, which I share with a nice woman named Nancy Cooper. "We sure are worried about you, honey," she says.

"Oh, I'm fine," I say, meaning: I am dying. "I'll be back here in six weeks. You'll never even know I was gone."

"We'll know you were gone." She has sad eyes, an edge of sorrow.

At lunch I take a walk. The day is clear and very cold, and I follow the feathers of my breath and feel the weakness in my heart. It does not take more than a block before I am breathing hard. I had thought I was only out of shape. Now, I am wounded, though a veteran of nothing. A few wisps of cirrus clouds blow into scallops over north Georgia. I categorize them into their physical structure, height, velocity, meteorological significance. Perhaps they hint at snow.

*

I get back to the office, and the phone is ringing, and it's the secretary for Dr. Vince Maffei, my surgeon. "Mr. Williams, we've had something of an emergency come up for Friday and Dr. Maffei was wondering if you'd mind postponing your surgery for a week," she says.

"What?" I feel my brain evading me.

"He said it wouldn't be a problem in your case at all," she continues cheerily. "A week won't make any difference." My mind begins to work again, and at first I feel resentful, sure that another week to think about things will lead me only to despair.

"A week," I say.

"Unh huh."

"Well, I guess so," I say. "It would be at the same time on the following Friday instead of this Friday?"

"Right."

"Okay, but could I come over sometime this week or early next week and talk to Dr. Maffei? I just want to know a little more about the surgery."

"I think we could do that," she says. Her voice is full of genuine empathy and it sets me at ease. (For a moment I think it has triggered an autonomic response that floods my system with endorphins—but the effect of slight euphoria does not last.)

She gives me a time early the next week, and I take it greedily and hang up, feeling as if the air has suddenly been sucked from the room. I hardly know what to feel, but as I sit very quietly for a moment I know it is a deep pleasure, almost a delight.

I will have an extra week before they stop my beating heart.

*

I have set my life in order a week too soon. My desk is spotless, old files thrown away, paper clips stowed, Post-It pads all stacked in a cabinet. I have nothing on my desk calendar except blank squares. Now what? It's slightly embarrassing to tell my boss that I'll be hanging around another few days, but I do it, and she is kind as always.

Later in the day, driving home, I watch the scudding clouds and think of Tolstoy for some reason, then of Russia, of the Rachmaninoff *Vespers* and the *Liturgy of St. John Chrysostom*, those deeply Russian works for unaccompanied chorus. They are contemplative, as I feel now. I stop at a light where South Milledge Avenue turns into U.S. 441 and look in the rearview mirror, but all I see are my own eyes.

*

I sit in the truck when I get home, thinking of my children, of Megan and Brandon, and for a long moment I hang there behind the silent engine, a small insect stuck in a large and entangling web. The bare limbs of winter hang out around me. The people who owned the house before us had a disabled child, and they built a long ramp to the front door for a wheelchair, and we have left it intact. Next to it an elm tree hugs the cold January soil. One year this tree shed its leaves in August, confused by drought into thinking the time had come to shut down its photosynthesis. Other years, the last small leaves do not flutter down until late October.

I am a fortunate man, for my children are by and large healthy, though Brandon suffers from a mild seizure disorder. I have lived until the age of forty-three without having to count my losses. And now this. But I am beginning to realize that a euphoria is running through my veins, a reprieve from hospitals and IVs and body shaving. There is a good chance they will be able to repair my valve, and then I'll be free of medicines and the need for therapy for what could be a long life. I would have cheated my biological clock, without guilt and certainly without regret.

I open the door of the Ford Ranger and get out and walk slowly across the yard toward the front door and my waiting wife. She's in the kitchen washing some dishes and listening to the radio. She teaches eighth-grade English, and all day she's away from the world, and by late afternoon she can't get enough news. She glances at me and asks how my day was. Megan is sitting in front of the television in the nearby great room watching "Barney" and trying to sing along.

"It was okay," I say. The words won't form easily in my

mouth. The sentence seems to be shaping itself in a foreign language, one I neither speak nor understand. Then, "They're postponing the surgery for a week."

"What?" She turns and looks at me directly, holding a spatula.

"They had some kind of emergency for this Friday and they wanted to postpone it for a week, and so I said yes," I say. "They said I wasn't an emergency or anything and that it wouldn't make a difference. That a week for me wouldn't make a difference."

"And a week would make a difference for this other person?"

"Yeah."

"I don't know about this."

"It gives us another week," I say, and the specific gravity of my words stuns even me, for they carry much more meaning than I think I meant. "It just means I don't have to do it quite yet."

Linda looks at me closely. She is deeply unsentimental, eminently practical, and she must see the relief in my eyes. She reads me like Braille, far more easily than I read her.

"Then that's good," she says finally. "You want a glass of wine?"

Amazingly, I do, and I sip it as we chat in the kitchen, where the fragrance of the hen she is cooking begins to fill the room.

*

That night, after Megan is in bed and I have spent some time with Brandon, I go to the piano and play for a long time, easy pieces by Corelli and Bach and Handel. I am working on a Chopin prelude, and it's coming along, though not very well. I am somewhat dyslexic with my piano, and I rarely ascend into that natural realm where hand and eye work together. I especially linger over the Chopin, and think of him dying slowly of tuberculosis, drowning day by day, living in the cold of Majorca with George Sand as he struggled with the notes.

And I think of old Bach, living to a ripe old age and hardly ever wasting a moment in what was a lifelong homage to God. On most of his manuscripts he inked the slogan SDG—*soli deo gloria*—to God alone be the glory. Bach suffered great tragedies in his life, the death of his wife and children, and yet his towering genius was undiminished by those sorrows.

I try to think of Chopin coughing his life away or Bach shouting at his recalcitrant choristers at the St. Thomaskirche, but all that comes to me is that I am dying and my fingers are unsure of which keys to play next.

*

I build a crackling blaze in our fieldstone fireplace. It's so easy. The first flash of heat feels wonderful on my face. The load of wood I bought is somewhat green, and so it explodes and crackles, hissing with hidden water. Not long before, it had been carrying out respiration and photosynthesis, and now it merely releases its energy into the room and up the chimney.

We decide to read and not watch television. I get back to Tolstoy, who is gambling his life away and pouring out the madness of his obsession in diaries. He cannot bear his wenching and gambling and cannot stop them, either. So he does the logical thing for a nineteenth-century man of aristocratic heritage: He joins the army. He wants to do something wonderful but cannot escape his human failings.

I want to doze by the fire and travel in dreams with Tolstoy to the Caucasus. I would listen to my life from a coach heading deeper into the mountains, into the snow.

Earthworms

I measure the stratigraphy of Wildcat Ridge from the earth's molten core to the galaxies millions of light-years away. If I own seven acres of surface, I also own the bedrock and the broth of minerals stewing in magma. I own the nimbus and the cirrus in their time over our land, and beyond that I own the constellations that turn in eyesight above us.

The word "own" is merely a trick of lexicography. We aspire to permanence, and so we make claims to land and air and rivers and even the stars. I own the body I wear. I walk through each of my days with it. I will lie down and sleep in its quiet curves when I am given up to memory.

Today I am not interested in magma, though, but in earthworms. I go to the edge of the forest and begin to dig with both of my hands, turning up crumbled leaf litter and the Gordian knot of roots. It is a hot day, a Saturday. A red-tailed hawk is crying ceaselessly down near the creek, and that delicate piercing shriek buoys me.

My brother Mark and I tried to dig a hole to China when we were boys. We gave up after a couple of hours and decided our pit was a foxhole. Little more than a decade after the end of World War II, we lay in it and attacked passing German troops, turning effortlessly from geography to war. I dig down through the roots, smelling the rich loam, popping thick and thicker strands until I begin to find caves. I know they are beneath me, and they know I am here, probing after them. They feel the vibrations of my hands tearing through the soil.

*

Science is finding that earthworms are far more important to soil health than anyone ever imagined before, despite Darwin's late-life investigations into them. My friend Paul Hendrix is an ecologist and an expert on earthworms, and he believes their importance to the ecosystem can hardly be overestimated. They provide tilth, of course, but they also change the mineral composition of the soil, making it more able to support the growth of seedlings that prevent the soil from washing away. I appreciate that elegant yin and yang. Yet who, beyond fishermen, gardeners, and ecologists, appreciates the earthworms?

*

I begin to find them, strand by strand. They want nothing to do with me, dig madly when my gigantic fingers approach. I pluck one plump specimen out and hold it in my hand, and it wiggles madly, a small bundle of nerve endings and purpose. I lean down and smell it and come away with the aroma of damp soil. The worm performs gymnastic moves in my palm, with half-twists and rollovers. What has it been doing this morning?

I drop the earthworm, and it dives into the soil I have turned back with my hands. In less than five seconds, it has disappeared from my awful touch.

*

There is a Bible of these creatures: *Earthworm Ecology and Biogeography of North America*. And yet we still know relatively little about the place of earthworms in ecosystems. Most of what scientists know comes from a few dozen European species, while we are ignorant of the rest of the five thousand species that inhabit earth's underworld.

Scientists already know that earthworms may selectively ingest high-quality residues, but the effect of worms on low-quality soil may be even more significant. There, worms fragment the residues, inoculate them with microbes, and incorporate them back into the soil. In fact, many species now found in North America originally came from Europe.

*

The study and classification of earthworms is nothing new. Linnaeus described them in his *Systema Naturae* (1758), and the history of their study has continued unabated until now. Darwin's elegant study was called *The Formation of Vegetable Mould Through the Action of Worms, with Observations on their Habits*. Still, one researcher in the *Earthworm Ecology* book has found that they may be undesirable for some agricultural systems. He said these effects include the removal or burial of surface residues that would otherwise protect soil surfaces from erosion and the riddling of irrigation ditches, making them less able to carry water.

Of all this, the earthworms are sublimely indifferent. Tests at the University of Georgia's Horseshoe Bend research area have discovered some four hundred to five hundred earthworms from as many as four different species in a single square meter of soil.

*

How do earthworms help plants grow, or do they? No one really knows. Do worms affect soil porosity and infiltration dramatically or only mildly? Ditto. Scientists do know that the earthworm populations in no-till agriculture sites are extremely high and clearly play an important role. About all we can say is that they are our largely unseen companions. They gauge us by the vibrations we make as we walk. Except for the back-yard gardener, few people have intimate encounters with the earthworm.

*

Wildcat Ridge must be filled with earthworms, because I fill my hands with them, hold them close to my ear to catch any sound. I hear the whisper of their motion against my cupped palm but nothing else that close. The distant sounds embroider the air here—the hawk, the crow, the jet three miles up gliding on its vapor trail.

I gird myself and touch the tip of my tongue to one particularly fat worm, and it tastes like soil smells. Has one of us introduced a bacterium to the other? I doubt it, don't worry in any case. I lay the worms back in the leaf litter and woodland soil, cover them over. I lean down and put my ear to the soil and try to hear them tunnel down and down. But it's just leaves above me, other sounds.

*

I have a lifelong obsession with caves and catacombs, with what is hidden. I even wrote a novel (*Blue Crystal*) about the cave country of Kentucky. Not a single reviewer noticed it was a retelling of the Polyphemus episode of *The Odyssey*. No matter. My natural state is concealment, which I understand. Paul Raeburn wrote a book about Hemingway called *Fame Became of Him*, which traces how the author used the mass media to become a public figure. He was a metaphorical eagle, strutting his wingspan and predatory nature.

I am closer to an earthworm. I want to dig down and stay there. I understand why Emily Dickinson kept indoors and lived through her imagination much better than I understand the "barbaric yawp" of a Norman Mailer.

*

If I try to understand earthworms, however, it is clear they have no use for me. We are too far apart on the phylogenetic scale to have anything in common. I love the Mammoth Cave system and have gone through some of it, and while there I imagined the great earthworms who might have carved those magnificent tunnels from limestone. (The natural process of rushing water through soft stone satisfies me intellectually, but my imagination begs for a better story.)

Do the worms of Wildcat Ridge have their own system of caves, even the ones which are ever collapsing and being rebuilt? Their world is not made of stone, and neither is mine.

Their world is soft and pliable, and they move through it like an owl sailing through the humid understory of a summer night.

I lie flat down above them in the leaves. I wonder if they can trace, by their heat or slight movement, my arms and legs. I wonder if they feel the distant drumming inside the cave of my own chest.

The Thing Itself

Quite unexpectedly, I am euphoric. There are now ten days until my heart surgery, and I decide to live each day with the most minute precision possible. I am still (in private moments) in mild despair with fear, but there are whole hours when I feel giddy with delay. After all, there is a fine chance my mitral valve is repairable. If the surgeon can fix it, I will have no need for long-term medication, which can bring its own problems.

I can stretch ten days into the distance between stars.

*

I go for my presurgery visit to Dr. Vince Maffei in his office not far from Athens Regional Hospital where he will cut me from chin to stomach. His secretary is pleasant, and I take a seat and start thumbing through a magazine. A gray-faced old man sits across the room from me, looking at his hands, which rest lapwards. He is weather-worn, leathery, the stuff of farms and sun. He never looks up. Jargon floods me. Is he pre-op (like me) or post-op? He doesn't look well at all, and he seems determined not to look up. At his side is an old woman who has the farm-wife look I know so well—patient, enduring, supportive through the years.

A man looking the picture of health comes strolling out from the back somewhere, Dr. Maffei trailing at his side looking cheerfully casual, a head of thick black hair nodding to a question the man has asked. The patient is clearly post-op and in good shape. His face has color, his gait balance.

Maffei shakes the man's hand, spins around, and heads back to his office just as the receptionist calls my name. I get up, and she comes for me. I assume we are going to an examining room, but instead she takes me to Dr. Maffei's modest office. I sit across from his desk and he stands and shakes hands across a coffee cup and some paper clips, a few papers.

"How's it going?" he asks.

"Fine," I say, then, "Well, not fine, I guess."

"Ahh, you're going to be okay, don't worry about it," he says. He slouches back in the chair comfortably. "You're what, next Friday now?"

"Right."

"Well, what can I do for you?"

I tell him I want to know what's going to happen to me in precise detail. He proceeds to describe the operation in detail, telling me how they will cut the breastbone and then pull my rib cage apart to expose my beating heart. They will then put me on the heart-lung machine while he cuts into the heart and either repairs the valve or cuts out the old one and sews in an artificial one.

"So I wouldn't get a pig valve?" I say.

"Nah," he says, shaking his head. "For people your age, we always go with the artificial ones, because the others have to be replaced from time to time. You don't need that."

"No. What exactly does an artificial valve look like?"

He gives me a learned but brief history of valves, ending with a description of the St. Jude valve, which is a carbon-alloy leaflet surrounded by a Teflon ring. This ring is sewn into the heart muscle itself and opens and closes with the pressure of blood flow.

"I got one here somewhere," he says, and he opens his desk drawer and pokes around, moving things out of the way, an act I find amusing and analogous to what he will be doing inside my chest. "Yeah. Here it is." He takes out a small circle of dark material, looks at it once, and then tosses it casually across the desk to me.

I catch it through a shaft of late-morning sunlight. His casual air, his nonchalance, his tossing of the heart valve must be calculated, because they make me a co-conspirator in all this. He isn't babying me or giving me dire warnings about setting my life in order. He's even yawning now, for crying out loud. The endorphins flood my blood stream in a happy rush. The valve itself is nothing, a circle with two pivoting leaflets held secure by a rod in the middle. And yet I am nearly breathless with the thought that one of these might be sewn into the middle of my chest.

"How long will one of these last?" I ask, fingering the delicate chain of life.

"Don't have any idea, but usually for the life of the patient," he says. "All goes well, you'll never have to fool with one of these. But I think we're going to be able to repair yours. The tests make it look like we can, but we won't know until we do the transesophageal electrocardiogram and look at the valve itself. We'll be able to tell right away then. If we can repair it, we'll do it, and that's all there is to it."

"What if you can't?"

"You'll get one of those," he says. "Then you'll have to take Coumadin."

"I heard of that—now what is it again? And take it for how long?"

"We say it's a blood thinner, but it's not," he says. "It prevents clots from forming. See, the valve would tend to let blood pool on it and clot, and then the clots could break loose. You don't want that."

"Heart attack or stroke."

"Yeah."

"So I would take it . . ."

"You'd have to take it for the rest of your life, but it's not a big deal," he continues. "You might bruise a bit more easily, something like that. And you'd have to make sure you never missed a pill. But it's pretty common. I'm telling you, this is going to be fine."

We chat about New Orleans for a while. He's a Cajun, and we talk about beignets and the French Quarter and the heat. He's not rushing me like most doctors. He's still slouching back in his desk chair when I toss him the St. Jude valve back, and he drops it in the drawer. He makes no effort at all to herd me out, so I ask him about what will happen minute by minute when they start the surgery.

He tells me. Then, "You're not going to remember most of it anyway."

"I'm not?"

"It's the anesthesia—you won't remember the stuff leading up to the surgery—you'll forget all that," he says. "Your memories will just fade out somewhere in pre-op."

"Good."

He grins. "You'll be fine."

*

I get up and he walks me to the door and out of it and pats me gently on the shoulder. His secretary is smiling at me as I come out. He turns and goes back to await his next patient.

"You're the novelist, aren't you?" she says pleasantly.

"I guess I am," I say.

"Well, you can write a book about this."

"I doubt that," I say, and I mean it.

*

It's a sunny day, not too cold for February. I walk to my green Ford Ranger truck and climb into the comfortable seat and settle back. Across the parking lot I can see, stolid and quiet, Athens Regional Medical Center. Thirty-five years before, my sister Laura Jane was born there when it was little more than a small city hospital. Now it sprawls, and the jackhammering of a new wing goes on incessantly.

I sit in the cab of the truck for some time, looking back over all the mistakes I've made, the stupid wrong turns, the trouble I have barely avoided. I don't have panic attacks, but I want to get away from here and do something solitary and comforting. I want to sit by a lake and watch the ripples of unseen bream as they flit upwards toward the light. I want to walk with the speed of turtles, into country.

On Wings

It's late summer on Wildcat Ridge, the dripping season. Even the huge outcropping of boulders halfway to the creek seems to glide on its damp moss. I am sitting on the boulders late in the afternoon, trying out my wings.

I have never loved flight as some men do. My own father built and crashed a wooden airplane in the 1930s and later became a glider pilot in the early parts of World War II before transferring out to another unit. Flight fascinates me, but I am stodgy and earthbound. When I'm on a commercial jet, I cringe when the flaps activate, when airspeed suddenly decreases. Once, coming out of the Dallas-Fort Worth airport heading back for Atlanta, we suddenly began to accelerate violently and climb several thousand feet. The cabin went deathly silent. No one breathed. From my seat, I had a spectacular view of the anvil-shaped thunderstorm we were trying to avoid.

Finally, after thirty minutes of banking and dodging, the captain came on and said it was clear all the way to Atlanta. Conversation erupted as if nothing had happened.

*

It's that way in the woods sometimes. I can arrive and the insects go silent, assessing. I've seen deer freeze and stand motionless for minutes until they know I mean them no harm. Today, though, the air is thick with conspiracies and water. The steamy sweat pours down my back in a constant rivulet. I hold my knees up to my chest as I sit on the boulder (eyes open for snakes) and look for the insects. Sometimes I don't see them at first, though they are audible. Mosquitoes welcome me, hum in my ears, say they don't mind what blood type I am. My Rh factor is irrelevant.

I begin to see wings. They move too quickly for taxonomy.

The dragonflies lilt, diaphanous, changing altitude constantly and rapidly. There are moths and flies, airborne beetles, ladybugs, butterflies. A wasp lands near me on the rock, taking ritual dance steps, not getting too close. It can hurt me if it is in the mood for sacrifice.

*

A primitive stonefly named *Allocapnia vivipara* was discovered by scientists from Penn State. Natives of the northeastern U.S., these stoneflies emerge from water-borne nymphs and come to rest on the surface of the stream. The researchers found that *A. vivipara* has wings but never flaps. When a gust of wind comes along, it lifts the flies and they are moved across the surface of the water.

Some two-thirds of all the species of insects known to exist in the past 350 million years are flying insects.

*

Aerodynamically, insects shouldn't be flying at all. Researchers at the University of Cambridge designed an elegant experiment to find out why the lift created by insect wings takes ungainly creatures such as bees into the air.

Warren Leary of the *New York Times* wrote this: "When flying . . . insects create whirling spirals of air above the front edges of their wings, providing extra lift. . . . The spiral of air clings horizontally to the leading edge of the wing and slides down from the base to the tip before being replaced with another vortex generated by the next downward flap."

A vortex. The researchers discovered it by putting large hawkmoths in a wind tunnel and filming them at high speeds with smoke trailing over their wings. The insects, it seems, create lift greater than their body weight.

*

A large mosquito senses me and lands on my neck, plunging its proboscis into that blood-rich highway of the human body. I am slower than normal to react, for the heat oppresses me. I swat it finally and reflexively look at my hand. My palm is smeared red with the debris of spindly legs, with the insect's last blood meal, perhaps including a small fraction of my own.

Even in biblical times, the shedding of blood was a deeply imbedded ritual, and it has survived as a central fact of Christianity. Whose blood is shed for whom? The mosquito understood neither that it had been born nor that it would die. Of course, it did not know sacrifice.

The blood in my hand probably came from a cow or a small mammal down by Wildcat Creek. I am realistic about mosquitoes, which carry disease as well as blood and even announce their annoying presence with a high-pitched whine. We know they are coming and begin our reflex swat. In my concentration on wings, I did not hear its announced intentions. I dust the splintered thorax on the large stone where I sit. A summer thunderstorm will wash it back down the mossy rock edge and into the soil.

*

The death of a single mosquito means little. Indeed, millions upon millions of insects die here every day, just as millions are born. Is a month-long lifespan seventy-five years in human terms?

It's night, a hot, airless evening, and my porch light is on. You can scarcely walk out the door without letting hundreds of winged insects swarm into the house. They bank and raid the light of a single 100-watt bulb. It is more than attraction somehow; it approaches the frenzy of worship, though it is really only disorientation.

I slip out the storm door and close it quickly behind me, and suddenly moths of many sizes and colors flutter across my eyes, my hands, my lips. It takes me a moment to walk through them to the other side of the porch, and they don't follow me. They go back to the porch light. I try to see the patterns in their flight, to follow the lift-angles of their wings, but it is impossible. I am suddenly intrigued by the application of chaos theory to moth flight and make a mental jotting to ask someone about it.

The large moths fly with the small ones. They bounce off the light, cannot get close enough to it, are desperate for it. Some days I feel that way about love and cannot hold my children or my wife near enough to satisfy my craving for affection. As a morning person, I cannot say I understand the night as well as I might, but I understand obsessive desire, as most of us do.

Thousands of wings are lifting here endlessly, bumping up against the miracle of a false sun.

*

All the world is filled with wings. We do not fly as moths do, but we solved those equations of lift nearly a century ago now. What a pitifully short time we have actually been in the air, even if we consider the eighteenth-century Parisian balloon flights! We are earthbound, bipedal. If I could find wings, I would not head across seas or far away with seasons. I would spend my life here on Wildcat Ridge. I have always known I will never go very high or very far, and I am content with it. I am filled with wonder at the strange country of wings.

Autumn

The balance begins to shift in early October. Wildcat Ridge turns red-gold and orange, buries itself in shed leaves, and the cool mornings are nearly soundless. White-tailed deer are moving, and often the fawns stand in clearings, stunned by wariness and light, absolutely without motion. Cold fronts sweep through in majestic succession. A cool rain drips off the elm tree by the house, and the ants head into their bunkers, seal off their mounds against the drops. The butterflies are nearly gone, and the robins do not show themselves, but the red-tailed hawks wheel and dive through a cobalt-blue sky. The underbrush begins to wither and shrink. Green anoles come out on bright days and sun themselves on a tree stump. A hickory tree pours its dazzling leaves in a fluid motion across the moving face of Wildcat Creek.

The Art of Waiting

The days drag past. I am no longer on the job, won't be back for nearly seven weeks. My desk is fanatically ordered, no Machiavellian conspiracies in the files or drawers. The top is even dust-free, ready for me to come back, or for the next occupant. I said my goodbyes, shook hands, tried to look cheerful. My friends gave me a sweatshirt with an operating room scene on the front. The caption: "All right, so he dropped the heart. The floor is clean."

I like it, promise myself I'll wear it when I come back.

Linda and I don't talk much about my upcoming surgery or convalescence. We avoid it, just as I avoid it with my children. I ask Brandon if he has any questions.

"No, not really," he says. He has dark blond hair and brown eyes, a slender young man of fifteen who plays guitar.

"I'm going to count on you to be the man of the house," I say, echoing the same line spoken millions of times in varying circumstances.

"I will be," he says.

I pay special attention to Megan, who is two-and-a-half. I hold her in my lap, read to her, play with her stuffed animals. She is all movement, dark brown hair and black eyes, always dancing, singing, talking.

"Daddy's going to be gone for a while," I whisper one night after I read to her.

"Okay," she says. She puts her hands over her face and suddenly pulls them away. "Boo!" She's off running, and I want to run with her, but not here, and not in this season. I want to be paddling through the steamy air of summer, well and improving.

I want to lead her on a merry chase from the crest of the ridge down to the creek.

*

I have read everything I can find about heart valves, about the heart, that metropolitan organ itself, and I am reassured that all will go well. But I am sinking into an impenetrable depression that will not lift. Writers live by their emotions and sometimes die by them. Exposing nerve and muscle to catch every sensation is addictive but dangerous. Perhaps there are many varieties of death, after all—many approaches to the end of things. My salvation has always been hard work and a refusal to travel long with failure. I deny it. I rebuild my life quickly after each disaster, like the fire ants of Wildcat Ridge, but this is different.

Just suppose that I can no longer write. What if, in some medieval scenario, I find that the heart *is* the seat of all emotions? What if I am no longer in touch with that vital center of my life?

What if the words no longer come? What if the *St. Matthew Passion* no longer moves me to tears? What if I cannot glide on the raw emotions evoked by Vermeer's light? Would my life, then, be over? I find the entire skein of thought silly and superstitious.

If the feelings do not come, if the words of Flaubert no longer move me, I will do what I have always done. I will take long walks in the woods, and I will wait. Yet waiting is not a virtue I have known well, and so I worry over it. I know well enough what I will do: Walk on Wildcat Ridge and look at the colors, listen to the insects and the receding footsteps of small mammals. Perhaps I should leave a thread, like Theseus, so I can find my way back. I worry far less about the heart than the head.

*

Now, it is two days before surgery, and I am packed already. I sit home alone in the den, staring at an unburning fireplace, trying to read more of Tolstoy, but his self-indulgence is too familiar these days. He gambles, he repents. He lies, he prostrates himself before God.

And what has my relation been to God these past years? I have been in hiding.

I have always been a churchgoer of one ilk or another, ardent or indifferent by turns, staying at one church long enough for familiarity but too short for intimacy. I have been going to a Presbyterian church for some time, and its pastor, Hunter Coleman, a marvelous minister and a warm man, says he's coming to pray with me when I'm in the hospital.

"I'd appreciate that, Hunter," I say. "I can use all the intercession I can get."

"I'll be there."

Faith has been difficult for me, and I have struggled against it as Prometheus struggled against his bonds on Aetna. I had denied my heritage, argued with the historic notions of God, quibbled with the divinity of Jesus. Science has sometimes led me to disbelief, especially when some conservative Christians act as if two thousand years of scientific discoveries never occurred. And yet in the farthest recesses of my memory and consciousness I feel a need for the same faith I have been inclined to mock. When I watched Bill Moyers' Public Television special on the hymn "Amazing Grace," I found myself crying, as much from a desire for that simple faith as my inability to grasp it.

I have been a sincere pilgrim. I feel certain I can at least claim that much. I have never forgotten a conversation I had with an acquaintance in my college days. We had been chatting about Kirkegaard, Bach, Nixon, and a thousand other things when I mentioned I was a churchgoer. His jaw quite literally dropped, and he began shaking his head. "You seem so bright," he said finally. "How could you be a Christian?"

I didn't testify or explain, didn't even try. I fled, at least metaphorically. I blushed and changed the subject.

*

It occurs to me that I must deal with faith and religion if I am to survive this experience, but I don't want to face something that feels like a preparation for Last Rites. I may covet prayers, but I don't want something maudlin or even mildly sentimental, for I will deny it.

But as I walk on Wildcat Ridge, as I spend the days of this life thinking of natural process, I begin to understand something beyond Self is inside me, an occasionally reachable place one might call God. And I know that in my tradition the ladder I can use to reach God is Jesus. Of course, I tell no one about this. Most people embrace religion when they or someone they love is sick. It is a response provoked by fear, and one I understand well enough, but I don't honor such demands for intercession as much as I might. I want faith to blind me. I want to feel again what I felt on that winter day when I was eight years old, when I stood in the dying light and felt the aura of the world crowd me with comfort and promise.

After the Fall

The seasons shift with a delicious subtlety in this part of north Georgia. Summer is a long time going, but I am pleased when the first sharp cold front drops the night-time temperatures into the low fifties.

I cannot imagine living in a place where the season changes only a little. I would go mad in south Florida or southern California, and I have never understood people who want to be in places where "the sun always shines." Sharp seasons are essential markers in my life, just as cycles of rain and sun bless me. Autumn on Wildcat Ridge can be a dazzling time, when high and deep-blue skies share the spectrum with the deep red of changing hickory leaves.

*

It makes biological sense to associate fall with death and spring with rebirth, but that comparison is largely based on leaves, which shed their chlorophyll, reveal their true colors, and float to the earth. Otherwise, fall is a time when the speed of life increases. The deer, in rut, seem to be moving everywhere, and we see them in our front yard or standing, with stunned eyes, beside the road. The squirrels and chipmunks seem well-nigh mad with pleasure over the falling fruit of the oaks and hickories. As the canopy begins to thin, the hawks creep closer from the fields, to hunt in the open spaces where the mice are moving.

Ticks and mosquitoes begin to fade somewhat, though they will be back in force come spring. Scientists worldwide are concerned about the loss of frogs from the habitat for reasons no one yet understands, though one theory is a protozoan parasite. But our frog-and-toad population seems abundant, especially the immature toads that seem to rise with the dew each morning, unseen until they make a short hop just below you.

The mushrooms seem only to increase in this season.

*

Some days I think Wildcat Ridge is glued together with fungi. We have puffballs, flat-capped mushrooms, molds, mildew, shelf fungi. They bloom like scallops along deadfall, all colors, varied shapes. They pop up in the lawn sometimes as fairy rings that appear overnight, like a spongy Stonehenge.

We are walking in Wildcat Creek, a late afternoon in September, on our regular expedition for quartz crystals and pottery sherds, which frequently wash up in the glittering backwash of the strong-running creek. Linda is the master of the hunt, refusing to leave until she has the best specimens. No matter what I find, she goes me one better. Always has. I rather enjoy her single-mindedness. I show her a small piece of quartz with a single shining facet, turning it in the sun, which filters low through the sourwoods.

"I got this," she says, and she pulls from her pocket a chunk of quartz covered with crystals.

I am about to genially trash her discovery when Megan interrupts. "What is *that*?"

It's a shelf fungus on a rotting log that juts from the creek bank. I tell her, lift her to see it. I have never seen anything quite so beautiful at the creek, dazzlingly delicate shapes in what seems brown felt. They sit up from the log like a series of small human ears, cupped for listening and turned to the west. A somewhat snaky tidal pool lies at the creek's edge, so we cannot get right at the log. Linda notes the fungus and heads off up the creek for the next specimen. I put Megan down, and she sloshes off in her rubber boots that she's managed to get filled with water.

I am not so ready to leave it, however, so I walk twenty yards to a sandy slope and come out of the creek and slowly make my way barefoot back to the log. I kneel before it. Leaves are coming down around us in a glorious procession of pale yellow and red.

The fungi catch the light, nearly glow. I marvel at the beauty and purpose of these humble fleshy petals. I don't anthropomorphize, at least not seriously, but I smile as a portmanteau word crowds me: *Mycolabia*.

Yes. If they look like ears, they also seem labia, which I instantly and ridiculously relate to Mother Earth. Perhaps everything means more than itself, but I rarely demand that of the world. In its variety and delight, it can be only a shelf fungus. That's enough most of the time.

*

While there are more than 1.5 million species of fungi, only about four hundred have been found to cause disease in humans and animals. All fungi come in two basic forms, molds or yeasts. Molds grow with long, threadlike filaments, while yeasts are characterized by solitary cells that reproduce by budding.

*

Why have I resisted studying fungal taxonomy? Probably more a lack of time than a lack of desire, but I do spend time among the mushrooms and molds here. If I have studied the rest of this place too much, I have enjoyed the fungi in my own amateur way.

Several years ago scientists reported what may be the largest single living organism on earth, a fungus covering several acres. I was delighted but not terribly surprised, because even on this small patch of forest soil the fungi are pervasive. They grow in shadow and sunlight, by the dampness of the creek and the aridity of our dirt road. They creep into books stored in the basement, staining spines and foxing pages. They climb trees, both the living and the dead.

*

Megan comes back down the path, and I lift her up to see the soft brown "ears" of fungus, my celebrated *mycolabia*.

"What is it?" she asks again, halfway between excitement and disgust.

"Just mushrooms," I say. "Aren't they pretty?"

"They sure are."

"You can almost see through them because of the sun being low."

"Are they poison?"

"I doubt it. I'm not going to eat one. Are you?"

"Nah. I'm going to look for crystals with Mom." And she's off, floating in the dying sunlight of autumn like a spore caught in the wind.

*

Fall is a usually a dry season here, but the fungi don't care. They grow anyway. The birds understand their jobs, too. On many mornings I see wedges of Canada geese beginning to move south, and that stately movement can stop me with its purposeful grandeur.

This is my season, when the heat releases us and the nights are so delicious you can almost sip them with a straw. No matter if we move on spores or wings or feet, it is the season for moving, for reinventing our hereditary claims.

Last Things

This is my last evening home. In the morning I will drive myself to the hospital and check in. I'll have a whole day before the surgeon cuts into my heart. I could have checked in the morning of the surgery, but that transition is too abrupt for me. I need the day to decompress, like a diver trying to avoid the bends after a deep dive.

The day is warm and still. Linda and Brandon are off to school. I have kept Megan home with me, and we play together. I sit on the floor and study her face and arms, her movements. There is a taxonomy of loss. I cannot bear the thought of separation from her, and often I will pick her up for a hug, and she smiles then squirms into limpness to get away. I am struggling against being maudlin, and I manage to keep focused. I train the light of my sorrow and fear inward, project my heart on her laughter.

I take her up to my study. All my life I dreamed of a study, not lined with cork like Proust's fabled retreat, but lined with books. Kafka wrote, "I think we read only the kind of books that wound and stab us." I believe he was utterly wrong. I want books of all bindings and talent. I want books to lean against me and spill words into my pockets.

I have everything from *Bleak House* by Dickens to multiple copies of my own books, in English and translations. My novel *The Heart of a Distant Forest* came out as *Djupt I En Fjärran Skog* in Swedish. My first line: "Morning is rising in silence." The Swedish first line: "Morogonen gryr och det är alldeles tyst." I once stumbled into a collection of turn-of-the-century novels, and now I have dozens, such as *The Patent Leather Kid* by Rupert Hughes and *Fortune's Fool* by Rafael Sabatini.

I was raised in a world of literature and music, and all my life

I have lived happily among it. If I know Beethoven and Wordsworth and Faulkner and Puccini, it is not because of my native
intelligence but because my parents gave me that gift from the
cradle. I have *Jean-Christophe* by Romain Rolland, a long novel
about the rise of a musician of genius. My father recommended
it to me when I was a teenager, and I inhaled it, *became* Jean-
Christophe and a devotee of Rolland. I can't read the book now
with those same eyes, so I don't bother. But I cannot live without a copy of the book. I have dozens of literary biographies,
the letters of Virginia Woolf, numerous autographed books. I
open *Apalachee Red* by Raymond Andrews.

I have been much haunted by Ray lately. He lived only a few
miles from me, and I hadn't seen him that summer of 1991,
which he'd spent in New York City. I had only talked to him
twice on the phone when he got back that fall. We chatted
about nothing important, spoke a bit about our literary projects. Mostly I chattered about our new daughter, whom we'd
named Megan. We made plans to meet on the following weekend. Never happened.

Ray put his life in order, making notes and placing them on
his belongings for proper disposition. Then, in the night, he
went outside, put the pistol to his head, and fired once. His
brother found him. I was shaken worse than I ever let on, because Ray was very nearly like a brother to me, and he was a
novelist. Our careers had begun together. When Linda and I
were publishing a literary magazine called *Ataraxia*, we were
the first to publish Ray's fiction.

Now he is dead, and none of us really knows the reason. I
put *Apalachee Red* away after only a moment. I can't take it. Instead, I pull out the least maudlin thing I can find: *Fear and
Loathing in Los Vegas*, which never fails to make me laugh.
Megan laughs and plays on the floor, looking at *The Adventure
of Danny Meadow Mouse* by Thornton Burgess.

    *

I need something to catalog, as Ludwig von Köchel did for Mozart's works. I need to make after-surgery plans. After all, I'll be home for six weeks before going back to work. Perhaps I'll begin my long-delayed book-length poem, a project in homage of *The Divine Comedy* and *The Odyssey*, two works that have been in my head for decades in varying translations. Maybe I'll try Proust again, going through the slow unraveling of *Swann's Way* and looking for Wagnerian leitmotifs. But I can't make plans. I feel valedictory in all things, and so I hold my daughter to me and tell her many times that I love her.

*

Night comes. Linda and Brandon are home from school, and I take care to act normally, to say little that would betray my fear. I talk to my parents on the phone, and they reassure me. They will be at the hospital, as will my brother Mark. My sister Laura Jane has called from Macon with good tidings and love.

I pack a suitcase.

"What do you think I'll need?" I ask Linda.

"Not much," she says. "They're going to take care of you. In a week you'll be home, and I can bring whatever you forget anyway. Pack light."

She always packs light, and I always take half my life when we travel, mostly three-inch-thick books to read. I pack light this time, except for my biography of Tolstoy, which I'll read during the day tomorrow and perhaps after my surgery if I feel up to it. I put Megan to bed, and she's a sprite, loving and sweet, completely ignorant of what is about to transpire. I bless that ignorance.

*

I have another man-to-man talk with Brandon, who seems far less worried than I am. Perhaps he's read the actuarial tables or had a conversation with the surgeon or read my charts. He's very bright—nothing would surprise me. I go outside for only a few minutes to take a look at the woods around us, to inhale the winter on Wildcat Ridge. I just want to make sure I know the shape of it all, that I can say with honesty that I have tried to understand.

It's quiet, not too cold, a brief wind.

*

I lie in bed in the darkness after the light is out and try to imagine the vertical slice, the breaking back of my ribs, the first sight of my damaged heart. I picture the transesophageal echocardiogram in progress. I memorize the stopping of my heart as Dr. Maffei shifts me to the heart-lung machine. I draw the cutting open of my heart.

I feel as vulnerable as a child, understand why those early years can shape or destroy us.

Linda goes to sleep quickly and easily, though she'll probably awaken in the dark later—she often does. All night she listens to talk radio with an earplug, demanding noise where I demand silence. From the night-light in the bathroom, I can see the shape of her shoulder, the rise and fall of her upper body in sleep.

I sleep only for periods of two hours or so, during which I have vivid dreams, often journeys of entrapment. And yet tonight I can't even fall asleep, can't feel the comfort of idleness or no great plans. I wish I had nothing important to do, no meetings, no surgeries. I wish I were younger, discovering books and music again for the first time, standing before *Guernica* in the Museum of Modern Art or listening to the Metropolitan Opera's production of *Die Meistersinger*. I wish I lived here five hundred years ago and walked through the Oconee River valley caring only about food and sleep.

Touching the Frost

A heavy frost has grown over Wildcat Ridge in the night. It's a sharply cool morning, and our yard is glazed, a sloping confectionery delight. I walk outside just after dawn and follow the feather of my breath up our long driveway to the dirt road. The air fills with wings and birdsong. A jay annoys another bird whose plumage I cannot see in the still-partially green canopy.

By now, the main breeding season for birds is over. The hedges and trees are full of old birds' nests, those elaborately sculpted cups that bring us such delight. Migrants are coming south. Some species feel even north Georgia is too cold, and they head downstate toward Florida. I have for years taken vacant birds' nests from their place in the shrubs and bushes and studied their architecture, and it is never less than staggering. The materials birds use are simply amazing—I once found a Juicy Fruit wrapper built deep into the fabric of a nest. The Carolina wrens here often get moss from our side yard (where the rainwater drains) to build their nests. Those fibers stay soft and green long after the nestlings have gone.

*

When Megan was four, I brought her outside on a frosty morning.

"Daddy!" she cried. "It snowed!"

"No, Sweetie, that's not snow. It's frost."

"It's snow! It's white, and it's snow!"

I tried telling her a fanciful story about Dew Fairies and the Frost Queen, but she simply refused to believe me and told Linda a few minutes later that it had snowed during the night. Virtually everyone in Georgia loves the snow, which must seem bizarre to someone from, say, Buffalo, but it happens so rarely that we find it somehow cozy and endearing—the Currier &

Ives picture postcard we never really knew. A heavy frost is not the same as snow, but that pervasive sense of white, slightly blinding, is somehow majestic all the same.

And so I let Megan think it was a small snow—not such a bad lie in a world where visions fade with each year we move away from childhood.

*

My neighbor's hill across the dirt road is sculpted in frost. The sky is a sharp blue. A jet two miles up scratches its signature against the dawn. I cannot decide whether to look in the sky or at the ivory expanse before me. Charles Darwin once noted that the average person rarely looks more than fifteen degrees above the horizon. I am no longer sure if this is true, but I could believe it, because most of us are hopelessly earthbound.

We have a long grassy strip next to the road, and I get down on my hands and knees and try to look as closely as I can at the frost, not even bothering now to look up ten degrees. I begin to laugh as soon as I put my nose close to the ground, because I wear bifocals and I find it nearly impossible to view the frost at a useful focal length.

I move my head up and down, as a scientist might move the barrel of a microscope, but I only see the sheen of ice, not its crystals. My breath fogs the ground under my hands, and I wonder for the first time if there's such a thing as breath-frost. And if I speak my name, will it freeze on the ruins of an ant hill and then return as a sigh when the sun melts it? We write very little of our lives upon the natural world, at least as individuals. We can strip-mine or pollute until the world is bare and dead, but words will never clear-cut a forest or drop snow upon an autumn hill in Georgia.

*

The colors change here overnight. In the best autumns, the tulip poplars and oaks are wild festivals of hue, while the cedars and pines hang green in the background. Sound moves more slowly in the heavy air. One might pretend it gives a solemnity to our outdoor proceedings, but I rarely get that far in my ruminations. I stay busy watching the elm tree beside the house to see if it is going to turn yellow this year or simply brown.

The trees use chlorophyll all spring and summer, but by deep autumn they are using chlorophyll faster than they make it, and the yellows and reds become visible in the leaves—unmasked, as it were.

I once began a short story about a man who changed color every fall. It was to be a piece of speculative fiction, snatched from the black-humor section of the avant-garde, but I got lost in plot, and the story faded away before I could write it. And yet I've carried that image with me for a long time—the man who changed colors. I had not even considered the racial implications, since I was stuck in the surface gloss of natural process.

In subtle ways, I suppose, we do change in the autumn, or at least I do. So far as I can tell, I don't change colors, but I feel a sense of escape from the summer heat and humidity. I ride the cold fronts like a surfer.

*

I walk across the road and up my neighbor's small hill, where the rime crunches beneath my boots. Everything green is stunned into submission. I don't need close vision to know that the ridge has changed overnight. The sun comes up full now, rising from somewhere, I fancy, near my brother's house a mile to the east. Surfaces dazzle me, and the rhizomatous world, with its miles of branching tendrils, seems unimportant.

Days like this are unquestionably in a major key. I have talked with music lovers for years about which colors they associate with which keys, and almost everybody has an answer. I have always thought of A-flat as being a red-scarlet color, and when I once suggested this to a musician, he said, "Well, that's pretty obvious."

Today seems to be in D major, that sunny and sharp key so

beloved by composers of the eighteenth and nineteenth centuries. Cold, rainy winter days are in C minor.

The grass, clothed in its hoarfrost, is still, but everything else seems to be moving in the wind, the last leaves, puddled water on the roadside, my hair. The light has a shimmering about it.

*

Autumn is the time for the casting of seeds. They travel by wind or water or through the digestive tracts of birds, but they are in motion through this season, a glory of natural process. In his book *Autumn Across America*, the naturalist Edwin Way Teale describes this delightful method of seed dispersal: "Travelers on the prairie in the early days were mystified by the great circles of plants like giant pixie rings. It developed that buffalo cows bedded down for the night in a circle, enclosing the calves, and in this position shook free from their shaggy manes seeds that had collected there during the day."

He goes on to note that a naturalist on Staten Island one autumn "examined two small turkey feathers that were being blown along the ground by the wind. Attached to both, ten to one and fourteen to the other, were the seeds of bidens or beggar-ticks."

Teale, in the same book, quotes a letter from famed naturalist John Muir, who wrote this to his sister: "I have not yet in all my wanderings found a person so free as myself. When in the woods, I sit for hours watching birds or squirrels or looking down into the faces of flowers without suffering any feeling of haste."

*

I kneel in the frost and rub my hands upon it. The cold is nearly painful, but I persist until I feel I know the ice by touch. By taste, it is water, and it has no smell. I hear a few avian chucklings, but I hear nothing from the frost.

Checking In

I awaken early on the day I must drive myself to the hospital. My small green suitcase is packed, and I am grimly ready to go through with this. I go up to my study and linger lovingly with the spines of several thousand books, play a few notes on my synthesizer keyboard.

From the window, I can see little of the winter, of the leafless slope of the ridge toward the creek. It stays dark for a long time these mornings. I touch a few things.

I open the middle drawer of my antique leather-topped desk and take one last look at the funeral and burial instructions I have handwritten. I shake my head: This is truly silly, and indicates a deepening depression. The odds are heavily in my favor, and I'm merely summoning drama to deal with it. In some perverse way, I almost hope for the glory of dying hors de combat, as it were, in fulfilling the family prophecy, even if a few weeks late. I feel rueful for a moment. This time tomorrow morning they'll be "prepping" me for the surgery. They will strip me of all my body hair and my dignity. They will save my life.

I feel a glimmer of scientific curiosity return and think of valves and blood vessels, of miracles and long lives. All along, I have seen myself as persisting to a ripe age, being a reclusive, white-bearded sage, a Whitman or a Longfellow (at least as critics thought of him before his reputation collapsed). I would sit by the red-and-yellow flames of a November fire with my grandchildren huddled around me, encomiums pouring in from all quarters.

Now, I may check out too early for any of it. Or not. I recall a line from William Carlos Williams to the effect that a man cannot die in midlife unless death has possessed his thoughts. My Uncle Sambo understood that well enough, and now I fear I am coming close to intimacy with it myself.

The idea of one's death can become seductive. I can imagine Ray Andrews struggling all summer with that idea, fighting against it and then giving in to the temptress, the siren of that long night. I can imagine him saying no no no no no no no no no no *yes*.

*

My family is bustling about, getting ready for school just like any normal day. I have already dressed Megan, and she's playing in the den on the carpet. Brandon is getting his backpack ready. Linda is moving around with last-minute things. I pick up Megan and carry her through the house, tickle her ribs, listen to the brief music of her laughter. I could write a *Concerto for Child's Laughter and Orchestra*, transcribe that sound into poetry. It fills me like a helium balloon, but she doesn't know, can't understand what is happening. I envy her that.

Finally, it's time. I'm leaving before they are, because I need to be at the hospital by eight to begin the check-in process. I announce it's time for me to go, and they come to the door with me. I'm wearing soft red flannel workout pants, a dark blue T-shirt, sneakers.

"You take care of everybody here, now," I say to Brandon, and I shake his hand and then hug him. He understands. He will grow to be a man of few words like Gary Cooper.

"Okay," he says, and he looks me square in the eye so I can believe it.

"See you soon, Sweetie," I say to Megan.

"And I'll see you after while." This is to my wife of twenty-one years, who will come to the hospital later in the afternoon to spend some time with me before surgery.

"See you there," she says. I hug her, pick up my suitcase, and walk out the door of my home, heading for a country I've never seen.

The Wildcat Mortuary

Linda, Megan, and I have gone out on this lovely day looking for the last wildflowers to identify. I have a book with color plates, and we've been puzzling for a long time over the shade of a daisy flebane. Linda and I have been up on the dirt road for a time when Megan comes running up the driveway. "There's a dead frog here!" she says. "I think it's dead. Come here and see it!" Her voice has an edge of anxiety to it. Autumn has arrived in Oconee County. The light lingers, even though it's past seven and a few fireflies have begun to flash softly in the undercanopy of the woods.

"Okay, just a minute," I say. She urges us on, running a few steps down the driveway and then back to us, like a puppy. The light, that fierce piercing blanket that was summer, is finally subdued. A slight breeze rises. Our driveway, like our house, is nestled in the woods, and it's darker here. Holly, hickory, water oak, persimmon, sweet gum, longleaf pine, red cedars, dog-woods—the forest is filled with the conifer and the deciduous.

"Where?" I ask.

"There," says Megan, pointing. She falls to her knees and looks at the toad, which I can see at a glance has died. I kneel and pick up a pine stick and flip it over on its back.

"Sweetie, it's dead," I say.

"Oh, no," she replies, deep sadness in her voice. "Let's bury it. I want to give it a funeral."

"That's not nature's way," I explain.

Linda is a few yards back, lingering. She is not a person with quick feet or intentions, preferring to take life slowly, to take life as a deliberate encounter. I stumble headlong into delight or disaster, depending on how much restraint I can summon. "Bury it!" she says. She can't take her dark brown eyes off of the motionless amphibian.

"We could," I say, "but that toad is going to make a good meal for some insects, you know. Let's leave him here. The ants and beetles will have a fine feast off it. That's the way it's supposed to be."

Megan stands, looking unsure, and I put my hand on her shoulder and we walk down the grass toward the house, though from time to time she glances backward.

*

In nature, death is continual. Hidden kingdoms rise and fall like the Incas or Maya, and we are dumb to chronicle that constant succession. I recently saw, on my father's back porch, the magnificent husk of an intact dragonfly. He found it on the porch and set it aside to study later. Its diaphanous wings still shine in the sharp light.

And yet, as Megan realized, there is no one to grieve for those millions dead—not for a mayfly, not for a toad, not for a raccoon. And that is proper. But if we cannot grieve over the constant cessation of life, we can do as I try to do—we can raise verbal pyres of praise.

My brother Mark and his family live barely a mile from us, closer to the Oconee River and also deep in the woods. I was at his house not long ago when I saw the husk of a dead cicada on his roof. "Look at that," I said, pointing.

"That was a big one," he replied.

And that was all. Insects, birds, people die, and yet life persists. As children, we come to terms with death in different ways. The sudden death by disease or mischance can change a child's life forever. I know that I was changed by my Uncle Sambo's sudden passing. When I saw him dead in his coffin, I was eight years old, tanned from a baseball summer, and he seemed asleep, but I knew that he would never awaken. Even worse is when someone is killed in a wreck or dies of a heart attack—that sudden, wrenching event stains us for years, if not forever.

Brandon's first death was that of my eighty-eight-year-old grandmother, and I was pleased that he chose to attend the funeral, that he saw her body lying sedately in its coffin. There was a natural progress to the death of his great-grandmother, a first death that must have made sense to him. I never knew a great-grandparent, and as I have said, my father's parents were both gone before I was born.

I have tried to teach Brandon and Megan that death is part of natural process and that we can respect it, but we should not despise or fear it. Some days, though, I don't feel very sure.

A few years back, our neighbor called and asked us to keep an eye out for her old black dog who was missing. I told her we would, and then I forgot about it. On a weekday after work I went to the creek and did as I have done innumerable times— I watched the dunes beneath the water, listened to the birds singing, slipped from my shoes, and walked upstream. The pebbles felt good to my leathery feet. (I never wore shoes from June until September as a child, except on Sundays, and so my feet are still as tough as old rawhide.) I had not gone a hundred yards when I saw the dog, lying peacefully on the sandy side of the creek, dead. I got out of the water and walked around it and saw that the dissolution of the body had already begun. I said, "Oh no," sadly, wondered if the old boy had simply laid down and died, here in the heart of the natural world, with the murmuring of water and wind in his ears.

When I got back to the house, I called my neighbor, and she sounded relieved to know at least, and the next day she and a friend retrieved the body and took it away for burial.

*

We think nothing of swatting a mosquito to death. Ditto with a stinging ant. And yet I have always tried to spare the life of any creature that wanders into my house or onto my arm. I came by this very early in life, when my father told me the story of Albert Schweitzer, at his home in Gabon where he served as a missionary, trapping flies to put them outside. That reverence for life moved me. To this day we trap moths, bats, birds, and crawling bugs and put them outside. For a time I tried to control the winter mice in our walls, but I gave it up. They cause us no harm, and if one gets inside, a cat does its job efficiently.

And yet Megan's instinct, when confronted by a dead toad, was to cast it in human terms. My instinct was the same. Once, when Brandon was about seven, he shot a mourning dove with his BB gun. He was instantly seized with remorse, and he made a stone mound on a sandbar in the creek, complete with a stick cross across the smooth pebbles. I did not see it until the next day, after he had tearfully confessed at night. In the context of my son's life and learning, the sight, in the early morning mist, was overwhelming to me.

*

A walkingstick has died. There are two thousand species of these odd creatures, though only ten live in North America. They can sit without moving for hour after hour to protect themselves from predators. The family *Phasmidae*.

This, I believe, is the North American Walkingstick (*Diapheremora femorata*), which lives in forests. The *Audubon Society Field Guide to North American Insects and Spiders* says: "When many females are dropping eggs, the sound is like the pitter-patter of light rain." I re-read that sentence several times, hardly able to believe it. Since I first knew of this, I have gone to the woods many times to listen, on clear days, for the "pitter-patter of light rain," but I've never heard it. Walkingsticks seem to be rare here—at least I cannot see them, which, I suppose, is nature's point.

This one has died in the front yard near Linda's bird feeder. I noticed it only because there was a dark patch of ants down there, so I squat to watch—never kneel near fire ants unless you want to be attacked. The walkingstick is dead but moving on a thousand feet as the ants begin to take it apart. They scissor off a mandible and carry it away like "natives" carrying ivory in an old Tarzan movie. They go after the head and the thorax, first taking off the antennae. I put my ear low to hear them singing as they work, but there is no sound, of course—at least none audible to my aging ears.

The tiny, elongated body goes next, cut cleanly into two pieces, and suddenly the insect is gone. I follow the train of ants back to their mound and see the workers handing the half-thorax along, taking it down inside the chambered nautilus of a mound. Outliers swarm around, looking for a foe to attack. They fold up the effort, retreat, disappear.

A few sentries remain. I like such economy, find it purposeful, even elegant. But death is easy the farther away we get from out own species. We all still cringe to see a dog dead in the road—a reflex of self-preservation I suppose we have developed over millions of years. I know many people who despise the human race think that everything we do is wrong, if not pure evil. Such thinking ebbs and flows, but as it does not contribute in the long run to the preservation of our species, I believe it cannot become widespread. Some will call me a mindless optimist for that statement, but I don't mean it philosophically. Biologically, we are not a little lower than the angels; we are mammals, and we preserve our own lives and the lives of those we love.

*

Nothing that dies on Wildcat Ridge lies alone for long. The crows come, or the buzzards, the beetles, or the ants. The dead are recycled. We mourn our losses, but the walkingsticks do not. Not far from here, I saw a possum that had been killed in the road. We have many possums here, and seeing one in the road is perfectly common. Their postmortem squires are the turkey vultures. I saw five of these creatures come flapping down in a leisurely cadre to eat the possum, and they cleaned it down to bone in less than an hour. Only a little was left, and the ants came and dissected the rest. I left and came back two hours later, and only scattered bones and a stain were left to mark where it had been run over.

Nature's way. And yet it seems we will never be entirely comfortable around death, for it triggers a deep response, a cascade of emotions that always leads back to the mirror. In that mirror, we see a creature that will die one day, no matter how good our doctors, our heart surgeons, our medications. That beast will pass, inevitably and irrevocably. And that knowledge spurs us to paint frescoes, compose symphonies, write novels.

Our knowledge that we will die is a superlative gift, one that makes us love, inspires us to create, gives us a reason to watch ants as they bless a walkingstick with a second life.

*

Megan is still not convinced we did the right thing with the dead toad. She thinks we should have buried it and given it a service. "We could have done that, and something that lives in the ground could have eaten it," she says.

"That's true," I admit, "but it's supposed to stop where it dies, Sweetie, because that's the order of things. People aren't toads, you know. You could still think kind thoughts for the toad. That would be kind of like a funeral for it. You could think of a nice plump toad sitting in the woods waiting for a fly to buzz by. You could think of its tongue shooting out and catching that fly—would you have a funeral for the fly?"

"Yuck."

"Then why would you have a funeral for the toad?"

"It's different. I can't explain it."

And so it is. The Wildcat Mortuary is a thriving business and always will be. We humans are the only ones who will be separated from this land and taken away.

Into the Heart

Leaving the World Behind

It's February 21, 1994, a warm and cloudy day. El Niño is caus-
ing this hideous weather, and only two days this month have
the temperatures been anywhere near normal. I love the bracing cold, despise warm winters, and so this day seems ominous,
if not downright sour.

I drive myself to Athens Regional Medical Center. The sky
is thickly overcast, the air heavy with water and omens. The
weather forecasters see thunderstorms coming in later. I like
thunderstorms, so that may be my only consolation. I park in
the high-rise lot across the street and slowly walk over, carrying my small green suitcase and the biography of Tolstoy. I
come in a side door, into the silence and fanatical cleanliness
of the hospital.

The check-in area is not yet open, but I am not surprised,
for I am a chronic early bird. I am accustomed to waiting for
awnings to be lifted, shades to be pulled up, doors to open. I am
not alone in the waiting area, though. An old man and a woman
I take to be his wife sit near me, and she is flipping through a
magazine casually while he stares straight ahead.

"They said eight, it's a minute after," says the man, who
is wearing overalls and is leathered, weather-tough, laconic.
He looks at his watch, which hangs loosely from a thin, liver-
spotted arm. He brings it to his eyes suspiciously, thumps it,
listens.

"It's got a bat'ry, hon, it don't tick," she says. "I told you that.
And it runs fast. You know it runs fast."

"It don't tick," he says helplessly. "It don't make a sound."

"Don't none a them tick no more," she says. "I told you that.
And it runs fast."

"Well, I reckon," he says. He drops his long ulna and stares ahead again. I cannot bear the silence even for a moment, so I open the biography of Tolstoy:

"Russia, for Tolstoy, was neither St. Petersburg nor Moscow, but Yasnaya Polyana." The latter is not a city but the name of his familial estate, a place far away from the towns, run on the backs of serfs, with a samovar always steaming in what was left of the house. (He had gambled part of it away, and it was dismantled and carried off, then reassembled.)

I think of Wildcat Ridge as my Yasnaya Polyana sometimes, though my world is subtropical in the summers and not remotely as cold. I read desultorily, and Turgenev has just given Tolstoy a copy of *Fathers and Sons* to read, and Tolstoy has fallen asleep while reading, which infuriates Turgenev and leads to a bitter argument. But I can't concentrate right now, not even on a favorite book, so I softly and silently close it.

*

I have preregistered for the surgery, so my check-in should not take very long, but it does anyway. When Admissions opens, I let the elderly couple go first, and he all but drags himself to the window, wristwatch hanging loose over his balled fist. They disappear in the back somewhere. I fill out what forms I haven't already done, read my name again and again. I laugh grimly thinking of my tombstone dates, knowing the first date and wondering about the last one.

All my life I have had abundant energy for almost any task, and I can even find reserves and tap them like an oil field. But today my passion is at a low ebb, and I can scarcely move the pen across the page.

After a time they come to get me and take me upstairs: I want to walk, but the black orderly insists I get in a wheelchair, so he takes my suitcase and I keep Tolstoy, and he wheels me through the increasingly busy lobby. A woman I take to be a volunteer at the information station smiles warmly at me as I pass, and for a moment I feel a tightness and a compassion in my chest, but I feel cold and distant again before we reach the elevators.

"What you gon' have did here?" asks the orderly pleasantly. He is thin and has a small, high-pitched voice.

"Open-heart surgery tomorrow," I say. "Just a valve thing."

"Bless you heart," he says. He pushes me into the elevator and then turns me around. "Don't you worry none, they do good work here, you be home and right as rain soon as you know it."

"I hope so."

"Hope ain't got nothing to do with it. You gone be fine. You in good hands here. Maybe I be the one to wheel you back out. Won't let you walk nowheres, Transportation got to come get you. You come in with nothing, go out with a bunch of flowers."

"May be," I say.

"You be fine, just fine," he says, and quite unexpectedly he pats me on the shoulder, and I feel a mixture of cold fear and pleasing endorphins flood my bloodstream. I like him a great deal, and I'll probably never see him again.

I can see myself being wheeled out among a crowd of friends and flowers, can see that either as very good or very bad news. I don't tell the orderly.

*

I have a private room, and I sit on the bed and turn on the television, scan a few channels, turn it off, check out the view from the window, unpack my suitcase, as if I were settling into a Holiday Inn and ready to slip into my trunks and hit the beach.

By this time tomorrow morning I will be in surgery. They will come for me at seven to prep me for the surgery at eight. I wonder what in the hell "prep" means anyway. I know they will give me a sedative to calm me before I am wheeled out. I know that I will be fully conscious when they begin the anesthesia but that I will not remember it. I know little else. I lie on the bed and try to read but give it up and listen to my heart and hate it. I hate the disease that has put me here, hate my grandfather and Uncle Sambo for having named me their heir. I am only technically forty-four, having celebrated my birthday on January 30. I cannot live in moments anymore. The time is at hand.

Lewis Grizzard, the writer from Atlanta, has recently died during heart surgery. He had valve disease, too. I never met him, but I feel his shade standing in the room, flipping quarters and whistling.

I hit myself on the chest again and again and again. Suddenly I am furious with my body, with my fear, with everything in my life. I don't feel sad, don't feel weepy. I want to hit someone very hard, to scream, to grab my own heart and squeeze it, shape it to my will.

I settle into a cold rage.

Too Young For This

After three-quarters of an hour, my rage subsides. I think of photographs of my grandfather who died at forty-three. He looked so old and worn out, exhausted from a brief life with a good family but without much money. How long was he sick before he died? No one really knows, except that he was bedridden for a week before he slipped away. I would give anything to hear him play a mountain breakdown on the fiddle, to hear him speak a few words so I could know what his voice sounded like.

And his wife, my grandmother, what of her? Dying at fifty-seven of stomach cancer nearly three years before I was born, suffering terrible agonies against which her deep faith in God must have sustained her—what of her? I have spent my life trying to imagine them, to tell them I am Woody's younger son, that I am trying to make something of my life.

I want to know they are proud of me. I want to get beyond the faces in black-and-white photographs, but I know I will not, shy of heaven. I will never see them in a film or hear their voices on a tape—they are the ghosts of memory.

*

I knew my mother's parents very well. Papa Sisk was a big, friendly man who, as the lovely old saying goes, "never met a stranger." He laughed frequently, told stories, took an occasional sip of whiskey from a pint bottle he hid from my grandmother. He loved baseball. When I was a boy and slept in the same bedroom with him on visits, we would listen to the St. Louis Cardinals, and he would tell me stories of Dizzy Dean, of the Gashouse Gang.

His heart killed him, too. In 1969, at the early age of seventy-one, he suffered a heart attack and died during the first manned moon landing, which he had followed closely. He lost his life the day after Neil Armstrong's "one small step for a man."

Mama Sisk lived well into her nineties, and I loved her as much as anyone on this earth. A quiet woman of great dignity and strength, she loved to read and kept a copy of my first novel on her nightstand. In her later years she moved, with little complaint, to a personal care home not far from me, and I was able to visit her often during the last two years of her life, when we became very close.

Once, I came into her room, and she was lying on her made bed, looking out the window. I asked her what she was doing.

"Looking out the window at the cars passing by, Philip," she said. (She was the only family member or friend who called me Philip instead of Phil, which made the name special.) "I watch them and imagine what they're doing, what they're like, where they're going. It's a nice way to pass the time."

I began to sob. I did not want to cry in front of her, so I turned away, coughed, and dried my eyes before turning back. What faith! What fortitude. She had lost her home, lost her furniture, lost her husband, and yet she refused to let her imagination fade. I have never forgotten that moment, remember it now as I sit in my ridiculous gown and look out the hospital window.

*

I am dying, of course, but this is a slow journey, a winter rain. No one picks out my window from the street, and there is no sun today to burn in my window like a flaming wick. I would like to remember James Dickey's poem about the hospital window behind which his father lay dying. The lives I do recall wrap me like a flannel shirt, warm and lightly healing.

Ten years before this, back when I was well and very young, I took the title for my first book from a poem of James Dickey, "The Lifeguard." I believe it was the first Dickey line ever used as a book title, and he was gracious and deeply pleased. I sent him a copy of the book on publication. "It's a special book," he said when we finally met, and I was filled with pride and unpardonable regret that he said it instead of writing it down.

I cannot see Brandon looking up to my room window and waving, because he is fifteen and as unsentimental as his mother. And yet I want someone on the street to know that I am here, that in the morning they will stop my heart from beating as it has since my fetal pulse began in the late spring of 1949.

*

The Cable News Network drones above me. Figure skater Tonya Harding is up to her tutu in all kinds of questionable doings. Her rival Nancy Kerrigan is shown again and again, crying in shock and pain after being assaulted. This is low comedy, trailer-park soap opera. Or is it life? We have basketball scores, the weather forecast, the news, over and over. In my room, women come and go. I want to write a pathetic final letter to my family, something that will make everyone feel even worse than they will if I die. I want to shake myself awake from this and check out of the hospital, as if I'm leaving a motel, heading home, the beach in my rearview mirror. I want to make some grand gesture, the kind struck for statues and photographs, but I don't even bother.

Linda's teaching, Brandon's at school, Megan's playing with blocks at her day care. My parents will be coming for the surgery, and for a moment I see my father, looking up at my hospital window, a reversal of the Dickey poem that might bear investigating. It is late morning. The rain has come, and I know it is too warm out there, sticky, not winter as it should be, ominous, even threatening. I could choose not to go through with this, but I will suck it up. My fear alternates with my anger like a county fair pinwheel, but they are imbalanced, spinning to one side and then another. I close my eyes and place my hands flat on my chest and fall into a troubled sleep, feeling in the fingertips a ragged beating in my heart.

Going Through with It

The rain has come. I am drowsy, wondering if I might read some of Tolstoy's story or check out CNN. Maybe some international cataclysm will prevent me from actually going through with this. I'm lazing when there's a knock on the door and a young man comes in and tells me he's taking me to x-ray, and before I am fully awake he's pushing me down the hall in a wheelchair, making small talk that volleys back without much effort. He ferries me to the service elevator and then downstairs, where I submit to the usual manipulations from the x-ray technician.

Nothing much comes to mind, but at last I'm awake enough to watch everything carefully and make a note of the cool room, the efficient directions, the dim lights. I'm through before I wonder where the operating room is. The fellow from Transportation takes me back to room 4219A.

Athens Regional is impressive in all respects, and as I settle back into my bed and look out the rainy window I know I am a lucky man. And yet I suspect that luck may be less involved than vigilance. If it had not been for my grandfather's death at forty-three and my uncle's demise at the same age, I might never have gotten that first physical at twenty-six that gave me this head start on the second half of life.

Most men simply don't want to be bothered until they are falling to pieces. If I had not had a regular checkup, had not had baseline echocardiogram information, I would surely have waited until I was much more seriously ill to see a doctor. I have done everything right, therefore, and at this moment I despise myself for it.

*

The day drones on. I read, put the book down, look at the sweep hands of the clock moving me toward my exile in the country of surgery. Tolstoy was forever beating his breast, admitting his sins, and running away, either to the Caucasus or Moscow or St. Petersburg, fleeing both debtors and doubt. Afraid, I take out the small red New Testament I have brought and read for a time from the Book of Matthew, and I take some comfort, but I have been at odds with God for so long that I'm not sure what I feel. I am instinctively a Christian, a believer, and a Protestant, but beyond that I argue with God over His existence, fume about starving children, mutter about hypocrisy.

I read verse after verse and realize that I have no clue what I am reading. Then I begin to whisper the verses to concentrate, and I want more than anything in this world to feel that epiphany I felt beneath the oak tree when I was eight years old. I want to feel the wind of a cold front freshen my skin and the light of the sun in its descent to fall upon me.

Nothing happens.

*

Hunter Coleman, the very pleasant minister of Central Presbyterian Church, comes in to pray with me, and I'm very glad to see him. He is a fine man, kind and smiling. We chat for a while about inconsequential things as he sits by my sickbed. Then he takes my hand and prays for me, and I feel genuine comfort. I am sorry when he has to leave.

*

I want to take a nap after my lunch, but I'm afraid of going to sleep, of awaking, of remembering. I try to write some verse on a notebook I have brought with me, but it's no good. My imagery is dark and full of storms. Also, the wrist bracelet with my vital stats distracts me terribly. I turn on the television and let it drone, watch it for an hour or so, turn it off. Finally, about four-thirty, there is a small knock on the door and Linda and Brandon come in smiling and waving.

"I'm glad to see y'all," I say. "If I don't die of heart disease, I may die of boredom."

*

Linda is full of stories about school and Megan. Brandon wanders around the room and looks out the window, doesn't say much. Then again, he never says very much. I am desperately glad he is here, would give my arm to see my daughter, but I know I can't for some days. The thought tears me up, and for a moment I feel choked, but I regain control rapidly.

Linda talks about the hot, humid weather for a February. She and I love the winter and grumble like a couple of eighty-year-olds when it's unseasonal. We chat about nothing in particular. The conversation waxes and wanes. She looks so alive, filled with routine life. Nothing seems sweeter at this moment to me than routine life. They tell me that within six weeks or so I'll be back to work, and I try to dream myself forward into that place, but I can't. Far too soon, they are saying goodbye, and I hug them both.

"I'll see you after the surgery," says Linda. "I'll be here."

"I will, too," I say. "Why don't you have the surgery and let me wait for you?"

"Can't do that," she says. "You got to do this one."

She kisses me lightly and I tell them to keep dry, and they are gone, not about to leave anymore, but gone, and I am alone in the room with my New Testament and my damned heart.

*

Supper, waiting. A nurse comes in and gives me a run-through about the surgery, about the medication they will give me to dull my senses before I go down in the morning. They will come to get me about seven. I won't eat or drink anything else. She tells me what it will be like when I awake. I thank her and watch some more television and realize that I want to flee from this place, that sleep is taking me over finally, that if I close my eyes I won't be here anymore, but in another place, a land of history and Salvador Dali imagery perhaps, but not here. I roll onto my side and hug a pillow and turn out the lights. It is not yet 10 P.M.

I cannot hear whether the rain falls or not.

Acceptably Low Rates

The doctor has ruled out a pig valve, which physicians in their elliptical know-it-all terminology call a porcine xenograft prosthesis. No, I'm too young for a PXP, so if I need a replacement, I'll be getting a St. Jude Medical (SJM) mechanical bileaflet prosthesis. The St. Jude valve is made of pyrolytic carbon with a double-velour Dacron sewing cuff.

The St. Jude valve is a magnificent little device that has saved the lives of thousands since it was first used in 1977. There have been only two other bileaflet valves, the Duromedics-Edwards and the Carbomedics. According to the book *Valvular Heart Disease*, "The Duromedics valve was withdrawn from the market after twelve leaflet escapes were reported in 20,000 implants." The Carbomedics is in use and has a slightly different closing angle than the St. Jude valve. The authors say limited information is available on this valve so far.

But the St. Jude valve is by far the most used bileaflet valve in North America, working properly in both lab studies and in humans. The book is direct: "It is durable, quiet, and has an acceptably low rate of thromboembolism."

To me, "acceptably low" means that it will always work well, and I will live to be ninety years old. That may be asking much, but at least I know I am a good candidate for the SJM, unlike the porcine xenograft, which works very well for some patients, especially older ones. During the day before my surgery I found that a man in his seventies is just across the hall, and he's having the same surgery I am. I'm too much of a coward to go commiserate, but the knowledge that someone thirty years older can have the surgery makes me feel somewhat foolish in my fear.

Still, I have been warned in writing that side effects from my surgery can include everything up to and including death, which is not comforting but necessary, I suppose. Anyway, I'm still hoping that Dr. Maffei can repair my damaged valve and won't have to stick an SJM into my living heart.

*

Children have this surgery. The elderly have this surgery. What was once experimental has in the past two decades become somewhat routine.

There are no mechanical valves for infants, so surgeons must in some make repairs when children are born with severe valvular disease. And pig valves work poorly in infants because they tend to calcify, especially in the mitral position. The Starr-Edwards, Bjork-Shiley, and St. Jude valves seem to work best in children (not infants). One problem is size, since only a few companies manufacture bileaflet valves under 19 millimeters.

Valve replacement in the elderly is much more touchy than it is in someone my age. Lung, kidney, and heart function all decline, making the surgeon's job far more precise and potentially complex. Extreme fluctuations of blood pressure during the surgery can be fatal. The elderly have more problems with blood clots during and after surgery than younger people. The arteries are less elastic in older folks.

And yet, miraculously, surgeons perform valve surgery on the elderly every day in this country with staggeringly fine levels of success. Only heaven and statisticians know how many elderly valve-surgery patients are out there now, leading happy lives.

*

I have known people who distrust the medical establishment with such powerful concentration that they suspect conspiracies everywhere. I have always believed a healthy skepticism is good, especially concerning government, but from more than a decade as a science writer I know that nothing gives me more confidence than replicated clinical trials. Occasionally they fail, give incomplete information, or are rigged, intentionally or otherwise, but the overwhelming majority of researchers and teachers in the medical field perform their work with profound seriousness and honesty.

I put my utter and complete trust in my doctors, but that doesn't stop me from worrying.

*

I awaken in my hospital bed the day of surgery. It is just before six in the morning, and I am thirsty, know I can drink nothing. I feel clammy and fearful. I get my pen and open the small notebook I've brought but haven't been able to use.

I write the following on a sheet of paper:

I love you Linda

I love you Brandon

I love you Megan

I fold the paper twice and slip it into my shaving kit and lie back on my bed and wait for the footsteps.

Behind the Curtain

The door to my hospital room opens, and a nurse comes in and gives me a pill. "This will help relax you before surgery," she says.

"Good," I say, lying back, "I could use some relaxing."

"You look young for heart surgery," she says.

"It's just for a valve repair," I reply.

"Oh. Well, don't worry, you'll do fine. Dr. Maffei's a wonderful surgeon."

"I like him," I say.

She is gone before the conversation, which has trailed away, can go any further. I have turned on two dim lights, and I begin to think of the pill-taking as Communion. I could only have a sip of water with it, and so I imagine the Body and Blood of Christ, thinking it might make me feel better, but it doesn't, not immediately.

*

The minutes tick past with a deep stillness. I do not turn on the television or look out the window. People will be going to work. Husbands and wives will be kissing goodbye, making plans, laughing at something a three-year-old says. Linda is now getting Brandon and Megan ready for school and day care respectively, and later she, along with my parents and brother Mark, will be coming over. Laura Jane, my sister, will come soon. She has a family, too, and lives at some distance in Macon.

There is nothing else for me to do. I know that I must have this surgery or I will die. There is no choice. I find prayer difficult, and I do it with my eyes open. I am trying not to quarrel with God because I need His mercy. I know that many people are praying for me. For a moment, I believe I am going to cry, but then I don't. I push it back, stave it off. I am thinking hard of my family, flashing up on a mental screen the smiling image of each one: small Megan with her laughing eyes; growing Brandon, fifteen and mad for video games; and Linda, patient, strong, holding everything together.

I see each one in turn, and close my eyes for a moment. When I open them I realize I'm smiling, and I know it's not an epiphany but the effect of the drugs, which have started to take hold. *Our lives are but a sleep and a forgetting.* I'm thinking of nothing in particular when a young black man suddenly comes into my room with a gurney.

"Mr. Williams, you ready?"

"Ready as I'll ever be."

"I heard that. Well, don't you worry. Did you get your medications, sir?"

"I did."

"Then we're ready to take you down to get prepped for your surgery."

He puts the gurney next to my bed and I slide over onto it, never sitting up, feeling curious, not especially frightened, wanting to remember everything. He rolls me into the hallway and then down it, much faster than I had anticipated, and I wonder if the nurses are looking at me—if they *know.* We get to the service elevator, and the orderly pushes me into it, hits the button, and we are going down.

"Warm out there today," he says lightly. "Rain, maybe some thunderstorms. Don't ever remember a February this warm."

"I hate warm winters," I say. "I like them cold."

"Well. Yes. But the cold hurt the bones of the old folk, you know. This, I mean this ain't much better."

"No."

The elevator door opens, and the orderly pushes me toward the operating room door, and I can see it, wonder if I will panic when the anesthesia starts, but I'm feeling drowsy now, somewhat indifferent, even blithe. My mouth is very dry, but I could almost whistle.

"This medicine really works," I say stupidly.

"It does," he says. "We ain't gone let you hurt or worry about nothing, now. Don't you worry one bit."

"I won't," I say. The words seem true. I want to buy him a beer, but I know I won't even remember his face after this is all over.

We go through the doors and inside, where it seems there is not another living soul. The room is freezing cold, but I'm only wearing a hospital gown and a sheet. I don't see anybody, and I thought it would be as busy as a fire-ant mound. It occurs to me that it's an hour before my surgery and no one should be here yet except those who will get me ready.

I give myself thirty seconds to go through routine facts. I have a will, have left burial instructions, have plenty of life insurance, and a wife who can survive my loss. What else? I close my eyes for a very brief prayer, which is mostly "God help me, Amen." I feel chatty. I want to be a model patient, to be helpful and courteous. The orderly pulls back a curtain and pushes me behind it and stops the gurney. Another male worker walks up into my field of vision.

"How's it going?" I ask.

*

I blink once and hear Linda's voice close to my ear. "Phil, it's all over," she whispers.

Surgery

DATE: 2-22-94

PREOPERATIVE DIAGNOSIS: Mitral regurgitation 4+

POSTOPERATIVE DIAGNOSIS: Floppy Barlow's valve with degenerated anterior and posterior leaflets with torn cord of midportion of posterior leaflet.

PROCEDURE PERFORMED: Mitral valve replacement with a No. 31 St. Jude valve.

SURGEON: Vincent J. Maffei, M.D.

FIRST ASST: Edward Shelton, PA.

ANESTHETIC: General endotracheal, James K. Wilson, M.D.

OPERATIVE SUMMARY: The patient is a 44-year-old male who presented with signs and symptoms consistent with progressive mitral regurgitation. Preoperative echocardiogram showed severe prolapse of especially the posterior leaflet with very redundant posterior leaflet and 3–4+ mitral regurgitation. Cardiac catheterization showed severe mitral regurgitation with normal coronary arteries and a very large left atrium . . .

*

Much later, in going over my records, I will imagine myself in that cold room, with the scalpel being drawn down the length of my chest, with my breastbone being pulled back, with the precise incision opening my heart. I have mused on the oddness of surgery, because in truth the only ones present are the surgeons and the assistants. The patient is not present in any real sense, nor are the waiting loved ones. Each must imagine the procedure, worry about the pathology, consider the alternatives.

Surgery forces us all into storytelling, as if we were sitting around a fire two thousand years ago and speaking of witches and demons, of saviors and heroes. We must imagine, and then we must speak. By that time my waiting was over, and I had gone into a sleep which must rival death. I felt nothing, and I remember nothing. One moment they were pulling the curtain back to prep me for surgery and the next my wife was speaking my name.

I have waited out the surgeries of others before, and the feeling is strange: a deep worry, a lostness, a profound desire to be still and say nothing. And hope also persists. Much later, a nurse told me that my parents would be models for those awaiting the results of serious surgery. They were calm and patient, understanding and forthright.

When I told my father this, he took no credit for it. "I wasn't worried," he said, "because I believe in the power of prayer."

*

What is it about prayer that gives us such strength? Call it intercession or medication, claim it from Christians, Jews, Buddhists, even diehard atheists. I know that I prayed for myself when I wrote the names of my wife and children on that sheet of paper and stuffed it in my shaving kit just before the orderly came to get me for surgery.

Many people were praying for me, and I cherished each word of each sentence, for I knew it was love made verbal. I did not feel especially chosen to survive, but I knew that love was flowing toward me, and I knew its power and strength.

Love makes a coward of fear.

*

And so, on that Thursday in February, I was split down the middle like a butcher-shop beef, flayed, and cut up. And the man who did it was saving my life, giving me back to my wife and children, to my mother and father and to Mark and Laura Jane. He was giving me back to my marvelous in-laws, Fred and Marie Rowley, who were also in the waiting room praying for me. He was giving me back to the green days of time.

I have thought in the years since the surgery that for quite some time I was, figuratively at least, dead for a couple of hours. My heart stopped beating when I was placed on the heart-lung machine. In technical terms, my future tombstone should read: 1950–1994; then, 1994– (final death date).

But one death is all we owe God, and mine would have to wait. I was going to live after all.

Awakening

"Phil? It's all over."

I hear my wife's voice and blink once, then close my eyes again. I'm lying in Intensive Care with an endotracheal tube down my throat, EKG patches over my chest, and two holes just below my diaphragm. A drain runs from one of them, the wires of a pacemaker from the other. A bandage covers my chest. I have a urinary catheter.

Linda had been in the waiting room and had gone off for a bite to eat when the nurse came and said that I could have a visitor or two. My parents and brother came in to see me, but I don't remember them at all. The first sound I will remember is that of Linda's voice when she comes in a few minutes later. I am disoriented and can hardly feel my body at all, sentient but unmoving. It takes me a very long time to open my eyes, and I think I will panic from the endotrach down my throat, but in truth it's calming, doing the breathing for me.

"Are you okay?" She is asking me to tell her I am fine. I nod and smile with my eyes, and it occurs to me that I might be all right. I want to ask about the operation, whether it was a success, if Dr. Maffei was able to repair the valve. I can't ask anything, of course.

Much later she will tell me, "You looked *so* bad right after surgery. Your face seemed swollen and red. I didn't like the way you looked at all."

*

Time isn't a measurable quantity fresh out of heart surgery. I fade in and out, on a pharmacy's worth of medication. I see Linda there, and then I'm asleep and I wake back up and only a few minutes have gone by. I doze off and wake up once more, and she's gone. I see my mother and father, and they look the same as always, strong and calm. The same for Linda's parents.

I blink again, and Dr. Maffei is standing in front of me, grinning and asking me how I feel. I manage to nod. He looks into my eyes and fiddles with a few things while his physician's assistant stands nearby. I know what he's going to tell me before he says it.

"We couldn't do the repair," he says. "The valve was in far worse shape than I thought it was. We did the transesophageal just before surgery, and there was no doubt the valve wasn't worth saving. So we went with a St. Jude valve. It's ticking away. Can you hear it?"

I listen for a moment, and I feel a rush of shock. There *is* a ticking in my chest, like a time bomb or an old alarm clock. I nod at him, and he tells me that I'm doing great, that in another day or so they'll move me to a regular room where I will continue to recover. I close my eyes and nod thankfully, and when I open them, nobody's around except the ICU nurses, who seem extremely busy. I fall asleep, and this time I am gone for a long, long time.

*

When I awaken, I have lost track of time. We operate on the diurnal imperative, but I suffer from sensory deprivation, can't tell if it's midday or midnight. I shift very slightly in my bonds like a man tied down for bad behavior or madness. The smell of Betadine is as strong as soy sauce from an open bottle, pungent and nose-twisting. I am reduced to eyes. The trach is still whispering my breath to me, and I feel relaxed about it, not having to raise my chest to inhale. I try to not to think of the gag reflex, that native impulse that keeps us from choking, but my mind is almost a clear slate. My chest feels tight, and I can hear my new valve ticking, but I am only uncomfortable, not in pain. I realize that I am drugged half-senseless and that the level of medicines has been superbly designed through years of trial and effort. I am neither addled nor hurting.

The light is low, as muted as photos from old nightclubs in the 1950s. The Intensive Care room is almost silent except for an occasional burst of low words from the nurses. One walks by and sees my eyes open and asks me if I am in pain, and I shake my head. No. She pulls back my sheet and looks me over. The sheet goes back up and she's off to the next patient.

What do I feel? A slowness, a small edge of fear, a desire to sleep or to awaken fully. I want reassurance. I wish for good reports, for dismissal.

*

I sleep, awaken again, find I am talking to someone. Is it the physician's assistant? I believe so, but I am groggy and cannot quite understand what is happening until he is pulling the endotracheal tube out of my throat, up, up, and out. My mouth feels terribly dry.

"Thanks," I say. My voice is dry, toneless, a dusty whisper.

"We're going to put in a nasal tube now," he says, and he does, and soon the oxygen is flowing into my sinus cavity, down into my trachea and lungs. The entire procedure has taken no more than five minutes. I feel as if I have done something of moment, and I try to speak, but the words break off and fall. Someone brings me a little water, and my mouth is like a desert beneath seasonal rains.

"Better?" he asks.

"Better" is all I can manage.

I doze off, awaken to the same world. I remember Linda's words: "Phil, it's all over." No, I think. It is not over.

Out of Intensive Care

I awaken feeling a bit hungry, not quite so disoriented. I feel as if I have been cast adrift in a lifeboat, that the shore or rescue could be near. I can't turn and look, so I pretend the lights at my back come from the sunshine.

Whisper-quiet nurses come by and check me, ask the same questions. I want to be smart, to be a good patient, and so try very hard to please them. They don't seem to notice all my efforts. Being an ICU nurse must be rewarding/ghastly, so I drop most of my efforts to be a good pupil. My hand hurts because there's an IV stuck in the back of it, taped tightly. I begin to be aware of curtains, of the sounds from other patients. I begin to realize that my terrors and depression have entered a new land today. The surgery is over. I do not have to fear that anymore. Now I am post-operative, and new risks abound, from internal bleeding to stroke or heart attack. Still, I feel hopeful.

I start thinking about one of my favorite paintings, *The Raft of the Medusa* by Theodore Gericault, a depiction of men lost from a ship named the *Medusa* and barely clinging to a life raft while hailing a ship that has come to rescue them. It was a true story, one filled with rumors of cannibalism, but Gericault's image of the terrors of being lost at the same time hope returns is magnificent and terrible.

Men about to be saved from shark-infested waters often say that the worst time was right before rescue. It would be far worse to die after having survived, after having come so far.

*

Dr. Maffei and his assistant come in sometime that morning, and they're relaxed and cheerful as usual. Do they realize how much demeanor means to a patient? Obviously. My admiration and gratitude are boundless, but for some reason I'm not very chatty.

Dr. Maffei checks my incision, asks questions about how I'm feeling, listens to my clicking heart. "Well, everything's looking great," he says, stepping back. "We'll get you moved to a regular room here after a while and start you on a liquid diet. We'll start you up walking around, too."

"Everything's okay?" I ask.

"Oh, yeah, you're going to do fine," he says. "We're going to get some of this stuff off of you." He pats me on the shoulder and leaves me to his assistant, who begins looking at the chest drainage tube and the pacemaker wires, both of which still enter my abdomen just below the diaphragm.

"This is going to be uncomfortable," says the assistant.

"Sounds like a euphemism," I say.

"It is," he admits. "Now, I want you to take a deep breath and hold it, okay?"

"Okay?"

"Ready? Now."

I take a breath, and he grabs the tube and wire and pulls my guts completely out of my body. The pain is ghastly, and in my weakened condition I cannot fight it, cannot really brace against it, and though it is over in less than ten seconds, I am breathless with shock. He also takes the urinary catheter from my penis, another siege of terrible pain.

"Sorry, I know that hurt," he says.

"Yeah," I gasp. "I'm all right."

I close my eyes as he cleans up the wounds a bit.

*

Finally, sometime during that day when I am still half asleep and do not know the time, they come and rescue me from ICU, prepare me to move to a private room, and if I were not so weak I might feel buoyant. My bed is rolled down one hall, and I see normal people for the first time—visitors, nurses, hospital workers, going through the steps of their lives—and I can only think that I want to be like them again.

I want to be playing with my little girl on the floor before the fireplace. I want to throw the baseball with my son. I want to hold my wife in my arms, have long talks with my mother and father, shoot the bull with Mark, talk to Laura Jane about her family and her life. No time soon. They take me into a room and help me into the bed, and the effort exhausts me.

*

I get to drink some juice and have Jell-O. The EKG patches are still all over me, and the nurses monitor me from the station in the hall. I doze under the influence of my medicines, awaken, speak to Linda, who has come late in the day to visit.

"Is there still weather?" I ask.

"Yes, there's still weather," she says. "Megan misses you, and so does Brandon. It was about fifty today, still too hot for February, if you ask me, but it's not sixty-five, anyway."

"I miss them."

I close my eyes, and Linda's gone, and I think I remember saying goodbye to her, but I'm not sure. I look up at the bag of medicine hanging from a portable rack, and I buzz for the nurse to help me stand and get to the bathroom. She comes in, and it takes me forever to get to my feet for the first time. I feel as if my innards are going to spill out. I stand finally and totter to the bathroom while she waits outside. I manage all right and she gets me at the bathroom door and escorts me back to bed.

*

During the night my heart rhythm changes. I came out of surgery with a regular, strong sinus rhythm, but at some point that all changed. I got what is called an atrial flutter, an irregular rhythm that is not uncommon after open-heart surgery but which is worrisome for the doctors. The next day Dr. Maffei starts me on digitalis, and he explains the problem. "You'll probably convert back in a day or two, so don't worry about it. This happens."

I want to convert worse than anything in the world, but I can actually feel the fluttery rhythm, and I feel a cold depression creeping over me. I know a positive attitude aids healing, but it is very hard, maybe as hard as anything in my life. I watch television for a while, and the Winter Olympics are on, but I feel ludicrously upset by the strength and grace of the athletes.

More than anything, I want to get back out to Wildcat Ridge, to escape my own cul-de-sac in natural process. I beg for escape, like a fly caught, web-bound.

Learning to Walk Again

Hours pass as days pass: hazy, full of small incidents. I am terrified of sleeping and now awakening, and so sleep is a slope I must slide down and then collapse upon before it comes. I am up walking in the corridors of the hospital every day, very slowly, weakly, painfully.

Friends arrive, and sometimes they make an impression, sometimes not. I try to be friendly and gracious, but the weakness of my body is unexpected and overwhelming. I cannot concentrate on television, much less on reading, which I can't do anyway because I have no strength to hold up even the smallest paperback. My hand is sore from the IV, and my chest aches dully.

Days bring a hope that rings false to me. Nights, when they awaken me from profound sleep and check me, inject me, are unspeakable. I dream of release, of hiking in distant lands where I have never been. Little by little, I start to regain my desire to live and to see my children, but post-operative time is much worse than I had imagined.

I practice sitting in a chair.

*

The time after major surgery is very hard for many reasons. Especially in heart-valve replacement, the heart and the body are becoming accustomed to having something foreign imbedded there. Then there's my flutter rhythm, which won't "convert" back to a normal sinus rhythm. Every time Dr. Magill or Dr. Maffei come in, they tell me I'm still in flutter, and I want to hit myself in the chest with an angry fist. For a time I try concentrating on heart rhythm, as if by will I might make its beating more normal, but no dice.

My days and nights get confused. I want to sleep all the time, and then nurses are awakening me, getting me up to walk, helping me to the bathroom, listening to my heart. I have utterly lost the human quality of embarrassment. I also realize that I have been shaved, chin to toes, including all my pubic hair, and my hairless state is profoundly weird. Rather than connecting it with youth and innocence, I feel as if I am body-bald, ancient, alien. When nurses check me, pull back my gown and expose me, I feel nothing, not even shame.

It is amazing how the body loses its allure when it is broken or diseased. I suppose it is an evolutionary reflex, but I don't care for it.

*

Some days are good. One afternoon when I am listening to the television drone, an old friend from the newspaper business, Lee Shearer, comes quietly into the room carrying a huge bag of detective books. I was Lee's editor at *The Athens Observer* when he introduced me to Robert B. Parker, James Crumley, and Stephen Greenleaf.

"Brought you some stuff to read," he says. Lee is a man of few words but a hell of a reporter and a very fine writer.

"Let me see," I say. And he takes out a few and spreads them on the bed. I cannot think of anything more calculated to take my mind off my problems, and I am deeply touched, though I don't tell him so. "Look at that. I sure do appreciate it, Lee."

"It's nothing," he says. "How you feeling?"

"Not dead," I say.

"Don't get dead," he says. "You'd be ugly dead."

"I'm pretty ugly alive," I say.

I think back to our years at the paper—Lee's at another newspaper now—when we worked too long, drank too much, lived too hard. That life never really suited me, and I was glad to escape, though it was bracing.

"You were always ugly anyway," he says.

Then, without much more fuss or conversation, he nods, stands up, puts his hands in his pockets, and is gone.

*

One night I am getting ready to go to the bathroom, which by now I can reach without help. A pretty young nurse named Summer had been attending me only a moment before, and so I have no immediate needs. I start to stand, and the tube to the IV on the back of my hand is suddenly caught, twisted, pulls out. Blood spurts from my hand like a gusher in an Oklahoma oil field. Blood goes everywhere, over my ridiculous gown, over the bed linens, onto the floor.

"Help, Summer!" I cry feebly. Then, louder, "Help, Summer!"

Three nurses come running into the room all at once and relax a little when they see I'm not having a heart attack or a stroke, put pressure on the back of my hand to stop the bleeding, and finally get the IV needle back into the vein. It hurts, but I hardly flinch. After they repair me, I use the bathroom and lie back down in time for a very nice woman to give me my sponge bath, which she does very slowly, speaking all the while about children and her world. Her medicine is better than any I have received. At the proper time, she hands me the sponge.

"I'll let you do down there," she says, and she turns away while I wash off my hairless pubic area. Afterward, with my IV secured, my bath accomplished, I feel better than I have in three days, and I luxuriate in an hour of deep sleep.

*

I have to learn walking all over again. The problem is that I feel atrophied all over, without muscle tone or will. My brain is atrophied. I remember things from the past few days only in fleeting pictures, and I need a Rosetta Stone to uncover the meaning of things. Why can I not remember the time just before surgery or going into the operating room? I know it's from the anesthesia or from the drugs I've been given, but no matter how hard I try to remember, the memory simply isn't there. It's been erased, or perhaps it never stuck at all.

Every day a nurse comes and gets me and tells me it's time to get up and walk. I know they are not trying to torment me, that all kinds of serious problems can develop from being overly sedentary after chest surgery, such as pneumonia. So here I am, without underwear, walking down the hall and trying to keep the back of my gown from gapping obscenely. On the old "Carol Burnett Show," the comedian Tim Conway sometimes played a very old man who shuffled along with tiny steps, looking down. That's me. I try for bigger, more manly steps, but they won't come, and I feel unstable.

For the first time in my life I know what it is like to be old, to be afraid of falling during the course of a normal walk. I want to feel the power and the blood course through my legs, but I'm too weak even to try it as an act of will. So I move very slowly down the hall, pushing my stand with me, its hanging bag of Heparin swinging back and forth.

I see others out walking after surgery, too, and I wonder if their hearts were cut open or just their viscera. Most of them are quite old, and they struggle just as I do, and I don't want to look at them, much less speak to them. I want to be left alone in my humiliation. I wish I were being stronger emotionally, that I was helping others over their fears and sense of deep isolation, but I am alone with my flutter rhythm and the fissure in my chest.

Some days I can manage only to go a few feet past the nurses' station, but on others I venture farther afield, even to another corridor or the atrium, where families are lying about, some sleeping, as they wait for word of loved ones on the surgical floor.

It becomes a challenge, and one day when I am clear-headed and determined I pretend I am Edmund Hillary heading to the top of Everest, the oxygen thin, my will strong, the world at my feet. No one notices my heroics.

*

Friends and family stop by for a few minutes and find me propped up in bed, doing nothing but listening to my heart and hoping its rhythm will convert. I try to be pleasant, to listen, to answer questions, the first of which is always "How are you feeling?"

I want to say, "Well, there's this hunk of foreign material in the center of my heart, and it's ticking like a clock, and I do believe it will make me quite mad before this is all over." But what I usually say is "Not bad." Or "I'm getting stronger."

One day after her work is over, Linda is telling me about her job as a schoolteacher, and I want to hear it, because I emphatically do not want to talk about my surgery anymore. She goes through the trials and joys of the day, and I realize that she has had no one to talk to, either, and I suddenly feel as if I have abandoned my family. Brandon has come by, and he's fine, the same, and he does not seem afraid for me.

"How's my Meggie?" I ask.

"Your Meggie's fine," says Linda, and she gives me a list of the funny things my daughter has done the past few days, and I feel so very far away from her. She cannot come to the surgery floor, and so I only look at her picture and re-create her voice.

*

Athens has a National Public Radio station, and I listen to classical music all day and try to reshape the notes to my new world. The music calms my savage breast somewhat, my completely shaved breast, and one morning I'm thinking of what I might want to write when this is all over. I know one thing. I will never write about open-heart surgery, because I have been too afraid and do not want to revisit such fear again. I want to write something warm and funny, something that will give readers a sense of peace or comfort. Then I wonder why I am making plans, because my heart is in a flutter rhythm and nothing has worked so far in getting me out of it. I have a horror of a sudden gasp, of nurses running, of the feeling of going warm all over and slowly, slowly, slowly falling.

*

I practice standing around my room when I'm not walking in the hall. My surgery was on Tuesday, and by Thursday the high is in the low fifties and the low back in the twenties, then it's warm one day and cold again. I watch the traffic out on Prince Avenue, see people heading for McDonald's before work.

My admiration for all the hospital workers grows day by day. I have always been afraid of hospitals, loathing them, but now I am more accustomed, and I begin to see how that world operates, and how they live on the spirit of helping those who are hurt or sick. I don't have a fraction of that altruism, and I am ashamed.

Now, I am looking out the window on my wobbly toddler's legs, and below me the world is moving on its wheels, in great moving masses of chrome and leather. I want to be out there with them, to do irresponsible things, to eat the wrong foods, to drive a bit too fast, to go some place very ugly or exquisitely beautiful.

I want to be normal, and yet I know that I will always have this ticking in my chest, that I will never be quite normal again, and I do not think I can bear it. I do not think I can awaken each day and live with this broken animal I have become.

Coming to Terms

It's a sunny Saturday, with a high of fifty-two and a low of twenty-nine. Four days since my open-heart surgery, I am still alive and not getting any stronger, though I am walking "vast" distances through the hospital now. Each day it's an act of sheer will and escape as I trudge very slowly down the hall, pushing my medicine pole (as I have come to call it) grimly alongside me.

I have come to covet images of freedom. I want to be a mountain man from the Rockies of the 1830s, leaving civilization behind, going for my own life alone. And yet that middle-aged fantasy will never take place, for now I am tethered to medicine and machinery for the rest of my life. If I want to keep living, I'll have to take my pills.

There are others walking in the City of the Sick. Here is a thin old man tottering on his stick-like legs; there, a fat woman of no distinct age shuffling along, puffing from the exertion. I do not see any children, any lovely young girls, any wives tenderly walking by broken husbands. Each of us is alone, full of dark dreams.

*

The food is very good, but I tire of it quickly. I think of toads eating the same bugs over and over and wonder how in the world they do it. For most of creation, variety isn't the spice of life; monotony is. But it wears me quickly. I also fret over the shift changes for the nurses. I rely on them far more than they can imagine, think of the call-button at bedside as my lifeline, my raft. I put a name on a face, and suddenly they change, and another one is there, asking if I need anything, taking my temperature, writing secret words on the paper in a clipboard.

I want to read but can't hold up my book and haven't asked Linda to bring me something else. My friend Lee's detective books are still in their bag—I don't have the energy to take one out. I barely have the strength to watch television. This is not what I expected. I expected pain and discomfort, the sutures in my chest, the medicines, the coming and going.

I did not expect this weakness or the sinking depression. For some reason, I thought that when the surgery was over I would be buoyant, relieved, like a kid getting through a high school play. I would get stronger mentally and physically day by day, and then I'd go home, triumphant and whole. But it isn't turning out that way yet, and it leaves me silent and sullen.

*

People come and go, and even years later I will not remember them all. An old friend from high school, Alvin White, is visiting family in the hospital, and he stops by to chat with me, and he will never know how much it means. I want to feel ashamed at the way I look, with my dirty hair and sponge-washed body, but I am losing that ability. Tomorrow I will shower for the first time, and I am afraid and excited about it.

Linda and Brandon come, and I suck up the stories of their lives as if it were my own blood, and I feed on them. Linda doesn't have any big news, just the daily motions of life, and I think, Oh! How lovely! How wonderful to go grocery shopping or to get gasoline at the Golden Pantry! I look at the photograph of my small daughter and dream of her arms.

Others drop by in groups or singly, for five minutes or fifteen. They don't know that now I tick like a clock and will until the day my heart stops. They don't know what the nights are like when I lie here alone and try to dream myself past all this, to return whole to my childhood and start over.

*

My Uncle Charles Sisk, my mother's younger brother, has driven down from Seneca, South Carolina, and I am more glad to see him than I can say. He has always been a cheerful, laughing man, thin and athletic, former World War II paratrooper who leaped into the Battle of the Bulge. We talk about golf and baseball, and for the first time in two weeks I laugh, though it hurts my chest. Everyone else in the room loves his hilarious stories, and I feel something knitting in me, some distant rumor of healing. He has a keen eye for the world's strange characters and tells stories full of odd detail. He is also deeply tenderhearted.

The sun streams in the window and lies on my bedspread like a sleeping cat, warming me, and I think: Yes. This is the way healing must begin—a feeling of contentment, with sun and friends. Before long, we are all laughing at the stories Charles tells, and I am holding my chest and saying, "You're going to make my heart come flying out into the room!"

I glimpse a new country—a place where I forget what is beating inside me.

*

My sister-in-law Gail Tarpley spends one night with me. She is a registered nurse and a close friend, and she sleeps in the chair next to my bed, and I feel really safe for the first time. She is warm and thoughtful. Later I will not be able to remember which night she came, but having my own private on-call nurse is marvelous, though not as special as having a dear friend by my side all night.

*

My heart is still in a flutter rhythm, and I feel a dread and sorrow. All day I have concentrated on making it "convert," change to a normal sinus rhythm. They are now giving me a drug called Quinidine, and they say that should help my heart rhythm change back. But I feel it—by God, I feel the flutter, the heart that won't beat right, and I am wondering if it will ever go back.

I can't make it change. I can't. Like a record skipping in the grooves, my heart beats and then skips, beats and then skips. So I pray to God to help me, and the night comes, and it is no different from when I came in, except it will be cold, with a low of twenty-nine. If I were home and strong, I'd be building a fire in our fieldstone fireplace.

No more fires. I won't be able to lift a log for weeks, and by then spring will have come to Wildcat Ridge.

*

I sleep fitfully, awaken to see the night-lights, to hear the nurses speaking softly in the hall. Then, for some reason, I slip off the precipice of dreams, let go and fall down, down, down until I am in a black place, not unlike the bourn of anesthesia.

I awaken, and it's sunny. I feel lazy, and I move slightly. I cannot move any other way because of the IV, the chest bandage, the multiple electrocardiogram patches that cover my chest. (They monitor me, wireless, from the nurses station.) I will get a shower today, and I don't feel any weaker, use a button to raise the bed until I am almost sitting. I look out the window for a long time, and a nurse comes in, and she's smiling. She takes my temperature, and we have a little chat about nothing in particular. She wants to tell me a secret.

"The doctor will tell you more about this but. . . ." She stops and does something, looking for a word. She is smiling at me. "Did you know you converted last night?"

"I did?"

"You did. Regular sinus rhythm now."

"Thank God."

"You're on your way now."

"I've wanted to be on my way." I say it flatly and simply, not meaning escape but the first steps on the "road to recovery," as the pervasive cliché has it.

"I know you're glad."

"I sure am."

My eyes fill with tears when she leaves, and I look at the sunny window, and I believe that an epiphany will come, but the feeling passes amid my tangle of wires and tubes.

Dr. Magill comes in, and Dr. Maffei, and they both give me the good news about my heart converting, and I can't hear it too often. I ask when they think I might be able to go home, and it's going to be two, maybe three more days. Until then, I must keep walking and walking, practice sitting in my room's chair.

"I'll do it," I say obediently.

"I'm glad you converted," says Dr. Magill, patting me on the leg.

I feel like a penitent in a tent revival, what with everyone talking about my conversion. When they leave, I get up and start walking down the halls.

*

Two days? Three days? I feel the blood begin to flow in my body, like water inflating a sunken sleeve. My muscles have no tone, but they are starting to remember. I take a shower, and my filthy hair is clear and shining. I flex my hands, do leg-raises on the bed.

Now, I not only want to convert, I want to graduate. I want the sanctity of home.

Discharge

Drugs I have been administered during my week in the hospital: Resteroil, Olcasa, Cefuroxime, Tenormin, Ativan, Temazepam, Lorazepam, Insulin, Nipride, Levophed, Ranitidine, Acetaminophen, Morphine, Heparin, Metoclopramide, Percocet, Zantac, Lasix, K-Dur, Reglan, Phenergan, and Darvocet. The list is dizzying, but I have paid little attention to drug names in the post-operative period. The nurses give you a handful of pills and a paper cup of water and you slosh them down. The only ones I have actually requested are the Percocets, which are fierce pain-fighters, but I've tried not to overdo them.

Today is Tuesday, March 1, 1994. Today my father comes for me.

*

I awaken, and it's going to be a pleasant day, a high in the upper fifties. I dress myself in the same red cotton exercise pants I wore into the hospital, feeling both excited and wary. I pack my small green suitcase. Linda has taken home most of the other stuff the day before—the many flowers and cards, the letters of good cheer.

They're supposed to dismiss me by nine, and I am ready, sitting in the chair an hour and a half before that, watching television and feeling the ticking in my chest. The post-operative period in heart-valve surgery can be tricky, and I know it, because the patient's body must find a way to balance its blood-clotting ability with the new valve. I will be taking Coumadin to keep the platelets from sticking, but there's always a danger some vascular debris might reach the brain and cause a stroke or a transient ischemic attack—a TIA or "little stroke."

The worst thing is that I have been having severe back and shoulder pain, which Dr. Maffei tells me is because of my breastbone being spread back during surgery. The brain receives pain signals from the site of the surgery and, misinterpreting where to send the actual pain, sends it at random places. My pain, when it comes, has been staggering, hideous. The first time, I thought I was having a heart attack.

Nurses come and go. They change shifts and schedules so frequently that I haven't gotten to know many well, but I thank the ones I remember. I thank a custodian who comes in to empty the trash. "I'm going home today," I say.

"I bet you ready, ain't you?"

"You have no idea. It'll be six weeks before I can go back to work, though."

"Where you work?"

"The university. I'm a science writer."

"You don't mean it."

"That's what I do."

"I declare."

I still have a chest drain, which is painful—I'll come back in a week to have it removed. And the bandage on my chest is constricting. When they have changed it, I looked down at my chest, and the scar is not what I expected—I thought it would be something hideous, some enormous, swollen line festering like a plow furrow, but it's only a slender line. They say the scar won't be especially ugly.

*

They don't come and they don't come. My father does. He is seventy-one years old and healthy as a horse, a man of medium height who wears his brown hair very short. He is largely bald on top and has a white beard that makes him look something like Robert E. Lee. His name is Marshall Woodson Williams, but everybody calls him Woody. In the best southern tradition,

I still call him Daddy, even though we are both getting some-what long in the tooth. He arrives at quarter till nine, and I tell him they haven't come yet.

I find myself oddly afraid to leave the hospital. What if something happens to me? What if I have a seizure or a stroke? Who will be around to help me or to answer my questions? I don't say any of this.

Daddy stands against the wall, and we make small talk. He's taking me home, because Linda needs to be at school with her students. He's going to spend the week with me during the days, and I can think of no one I'd rather stay with. We can have endless discussions about almost anything. We cheerfully dis-agree about many things, especially politics. For thirty years I've been the moderate and he the rock-ribbed Goldwater con-servative. We can argue fiercely, and my mother can't stand it when we do, but it has never interfered with our friendship.

Today I don't feel like arguing. I feel edgy, though—worried, depressed. I thought I would feel elation, but I don't.

　　　*

Finally they come in order, and Dr. Magill tells me that I'm going to be just fine. I'll see him once a week for a while, and I can call him if I have problems. I like him immensely, trust him. Dr. Maffei's not long behind Magill, and he's his usual smiling chipper self, positive and encouraging. Everyone has told me he is a very fine heart surgeon, and I believe it. If I can't see in-side my own heart, I can see into his eyes. He's a kind man, and he has saved my life. If he told me to hop home on one leg I'd do it without question.

The nurse comes in and works for a long time on a discharge form. She gives me instructions for medicines. Under mental status, she checks "alert" and "oriented," and that seems to be stretching it a little.

"Now, you have an appointment on March 17 with Dr. Magill and then on March 23 with Dr. Maffei," she says. "And here are their numbers if you need them." She writes two phone numbers on the form. "You have Darvocet if needed for pain, and here are your prescriptions." She hands me the sheets the doctors have filled out, and tells me again about what I'll be taking.

"I sure do appreciate y'all taking care of me," I say.

"Our pleasure."

*

The guy from Transportation takes forever to get to the room with a wheelchair. I dawdle, turn off the television, wonder how long it will be until I'm strong enough to hold the Tolstoy biography again. Finally a slender black man arrives pushing a wheelchair, and I know that I'm going home. I'm wearing sneakers, the first time since February 21 I've had shoes of any kind on my feet, and I stand and walk toward the wheelchair, ready to leave.

"I'm sorry it took so long, but we've had so many people to discharge today," he says. "Lots of folks going home."

"That's all right," I say.

"I'll go pull the car around," says my father, and he leaves before us. It takes the young man a moment to get me situated in the chair and to turn me into the hallway. A series of postoperative men and women are shuffling grimly down the hall, and for the first time I think of the goodbye note I stuffed in my shaving kit, of the funeral instructions in the drawer of my desk at home.

I can't get the smell of Betadine out of my nostrils. I feel worried, fragile, irritated, unhappy. Since I did not expect this at all, I try to blank out my feelings, and the result is that I rest in the tension of forgetfulness and knowing. The young man rolls me to the elevator, and we go down four floors and then out into the lobby, and I realize with a shock that I will feel the outside air for the first time in ten days.

My father's car is already at the curb, and he is smiling, has the door open, ready to drive me home. I live about seventeen miles south of Athens Regional, and soon I'll be heading for the sinecure of Wildcat Ridge.

"You in all right?" asks my father when I've finally, slowly, folded myself down into the seat.

"I'm in," I say. "Let's go home."

It is a cool, partly cloudy day. I am holding a pillow between my chest and the seat belt because of my long scar and the drainage bag still attached to me. My father is chatting about a hundred things. We pull out of the parking lot, turn east on Prince Avenue, heading home.

A Time to Live

Winter

Wildcat Ridge shifts to gray, and there is a soft thud as falling

hickory nuts land on beds of moss. A cold rain sprinkled

with flakes falls, fades away. A squirrel pauses limbward.

Cathedrals of hoarfrost push upward from a cold night. Some

days a thin sun warms the broom sedge, and a neighbor's dog

lies alone with warming flanks. Orion straddles a sky where

vast depths of field move inward, outward, from a hill across

the dirt road. Raccoon tracks still come to the creek-side, their

splayed impressions filled with shallow and lightly frozen

water. A whiff of woodsmoke. Snow thunder. Sleet tapping

on the dead leaves like wedding rice. The road sinks in its

muddy ruts, and Canada geese wedge above the pines, no

plans for landing soon. A daughter's cheeks growing pink as

she leans against the wind.

Storms

The cold rain begins just after noon. It's about two years before my surgery. At first it's nothing unusual, just a pelting rainfall that comes straight down. The old folks would say it's a frog-strangler, that it's coming down in buckets, but there's more to it this time. A low-pressure system that has spent the week idly deepening in the Gulf of Mexico is slowly moving northward, its center visible on satellite photographs like the hole in a doughnut.

"Boy, look at that," I say to Linda as I stare out the open front door.

"It's called rain," she says, not looking up from her book.

All morning it falls steadily, hard, without slackening and without much wind. There is no lightning or attendant thunder. The world is gray, as we are in winter, but not very cold. Tree limbs drip, my gutters overflow and drip, my dogs drip when I go out late in the day to feed them. Rain falls straight down until darkness, and then it rains into the night.

*

The next day I go to work, and it rains all day in Athens, filling gutters, backing up drainpipes. As I drive home I note the Middle Oconee River is rising rapidly, a muddy torrent beneath a concrete bridge. Cars wipe the rain from their windshields, but it's very hard to see. The rain is heavy now and will not pass or slacken. I begin to feel like a character in *Rain* by Somerset Maugham, watching the tropical downpour go on for days and days. I stop at the Watkinsville Post Office to get the mail, and when I climb down from my truck I get soaked before I can get inside and get my key out of my khakis.

"It's 'posed to do this two more days, you ever hear of sech a thing?" asks an old man standing inside.

"It's a frog-strangler," I say.

"My daddy'd say that," he replies. He doesn't go out, just stands by the window watching the rain and shaking his head. I have a circular from Kmart, two bills, and an offer on insurance I don't need. Most of it goes in the trash can. I run back to the truck, and when I finally slam the door I find that my bill from the Walton Electric Membership Corporation is dripping wet.

I look at the countryside as I drive slowly down Highway 15, turn left on Flat Rock Road, and head toward home. It is gray and brown and filling. Cows sit kneeward, chewing their cuds. Not a single Hereford-cross, not a single Beefmaster, not a single Holstein—not a cow stands. I slow down because the road is slippery and I don't want to hydroplane. The ditches alongside the road are spilling out, completely full.

We live so high up Wildcat Ridge that the creek could never get up here, but as I cross it I see a rising and roaring torrent, and the drive up the dirt road toward home is treacherous. My family is already home, and I come into the house holding my dripping bills and a look of amazement.

"Did you start building an ark yet?" I ask Linda. She's in the kitchen getting dinner ready. (Every night for more than twenty years she's cooked and I have washed.)

"Did you see the creek?" she asks. She's listening to WSB-AM from Atlanta on a small radio, and it crackles with information and static.

"Drove over it," I say. "It's coming up fast."

"Go out there on the porch and look down at it," she says, pouring uncooked rice into a pot of boiling water. I hug Megan and shout greetings at Brandon, who's upstairs playing video games in his bedroom, and then I get my piece of a black umbrella and go out on the porch. The creek is stunningly high, and I know that it's filled with moving debris, flotsam and jetsam, and that the deadfall is lumbering downstream, the huge logs, the trees. Normally fifteen feet across and no more than half a foot deep, this is no longer a creek but a river or slow-moving lake. I estimate it to be fifteen feet deep and seventy feet across.

"I never saw anything like that," I say, coming back in and dripping water all over the linoleum.

"May not quit until Thursday," Linda says. "Go tell Brandon to come to dinner."

*

The rain falls relentlessly through the night. I know what is happening, that the creek is being resculpted as it has been for many centuries. The sand there three days ago may be miles down the Oconee River by now. Raccoons that wash their food in the soft swish of the creek must be watching from trees, amazed. My neighbor told me once that when the creek's in flood huge fish swim upstream from the river, and Brandon told me once that he and a friend saw a foot-long fish flapping in the shallows a few days after the creek was in flood.

By the next afternoon a field that borders the creek down on Oliver Bridge Road is a lake. The water rushes not five feet below the bridge, and I decide to go another way to work. When I get home that evening, the rain is starting to slacken, but the creek continues to rise.

I get up early the next morning and go outside, and look through the dim light and see a sight I will long recall: Wildcat Creek is now thirty feet deep and a hundred feet wide, and it seems utterly still, unmoving. I slip into my heavy boots and jeans and walk down the paths through the forest and stop at the edge of the water. I do not see familiar marks. The rain has stopped finally, and birds are crying and swooping. The air is very still and quite cold. The movement of water, like the motion of air, is imperceptible. I lean against an oak. The majestic beech trees that line the creek bank are up to their armpits in water.

*

It takes five days for the creek to entirely recede, and I find that the channel has changed. Huge logs there for two years have vanished, and a thick coating of mud covers the sandbars.

"I could find a crystal in that if you gave me time," says Linda as we look it over.

How many times has Wildcat Creek seen this same rising and falling? Hundreds? Thousands? The event is marvelous to me.

Marcus Aurelius wrote: "The safety of life is this, to examine everything all through, what it is itself, what is its material, what the formal part; with all thy soul to do justice and to say the truth. What remains except to enjoy life by joining one good thing to another so as not to leave even the smallest intervals between."

Coming Home

The streets of Athens peel back behind me as my father drives me from the hospital south toward Oconee County and home. I want to feel exultant, but I am fragile, shockingly weak, and I have almost no strength, even for small talk. Some weeks before, I had been having the latest installment of a lifetime discussion with Daddy about the greatest composers and the greatest compositions, and as usual he was pushing for Mozart. I replayed my claim for Johann Sebastian Bach, whom I believe was the greatest creative genius who ever walked the earth. We became stalled, however, at the comparative merits of the slow movement of the Bach *Concerto for Two Violins and Orchestra* and the Mozart *Clarinet Quintet*, he arguing for the latter, I for the former.

"To me, the slow movement of the double violin concerto is the single most beautiful piece of music ever written," I said.

Now, as we head home, he has inserted a cassette into the car stereo, and knowing my father as a sometimes sentimental man, I understand he is trying to play my slow movement for me as a lovely segue into the still winter-struck countryside. Except he can't get the tape cued up.

"Don't worry about it," I say hoarsely as we pass through Watkinsville and turn onto Flat Rock Road.

"It's right here somewhere," he says, driving with one hand and fast-forwarding with the other. It's on the fourth or fifth attempt to locate the piece that I begin to feel the pain growing behind my left shoulder. At first it's dull and distant, but every second it intensifies until I am in ghastly pain and begin to writhe and moan, think I may burst into tears.

"Are you all right?" he asks.

"No," I say. "I'm not."

"Do you want me to pull over?"

"Yes," I reply, and then I emit a groan from somewhere "too deep for tears," and we are pulling off the road.

*

I lean forward in my seat as he comes around and rubs my shoulder. I try to be precise in my thinking, to determine if it's a heart attack, but I know it's not. They've told me it's pain that comes from having my sternum spread back, that it could continue for days or weeks. We have stopped at the edge of a spreading pasture, and I groan in pain for two or three minutes before it begins to subside.

"Okay, I think it's getting better now," I say.

"Ready to go?"

"Yeah."

Daddy closes the door and comes around and miraculously finds the slow movement he's been seeking, and the rest of the way home I listen to Bach. Our house is on a dirt road that heads steeply uphill, a road that's been rutted from winter rain, and we bounce over it slowly. I feel each jolt in my joints, each dip in the wires that hold my chest together. (Even breathing, I can feel the halves of my chest moving at slightly different angles, so I know that the bone has not knit.)

It is late winter on Wildcat Ridge, almost spring. By early March the jonquils are blooming, and the cold weather starts to recede, and on this day the world seems to shimmer with a new light, but I don't feel it very far down. I am not even sure I can walk all the way from the car to the front door without collapsing.

We park out front, and I am pleased to be here but worried that another attack will take me down. There is almost nothing inside me. I hear my heart ticking in the silence of the car as Daddy comes around to open the door and help me out. It is an odd feeling to be a forty-four-year-old man and be helped by your father as if you were eighty. This peculiar role reversal is something I navigate lightly, and I do not dislike it. I am lucky that he is retired and comes to stay with me each day. He has come bearing a bag full of old movies on videotape.

The family who owned the house before us had a handicapped child, and we left the wheelchair ramp when we moved in, a ramp more like a bridge that anything else, and now my father helps me walk very slowly across the grass and onto the bridge and then to the front porch. Once inside, I collapse on the sofa, and for the first time I feel a vast delight in being home.

*

The day passes slowly, and we watch a movie called *The Next Voice You Hear*, a Second-Coming fable from the 1940s that I find very touching. I doze, awaken, want to go to my study upstairs, but I know I do not have the strength to climb stairs, may not for many days. It will be six weeks before I can go back to work, at least three weeks before I can leave my own yard. We eat sandwiches and talk, listen to some Brahms on the stereo, even have a brief feint at politics, about which we always cheerfully disagree. But my heart, as it were, is not in the fight.

I can only think of one thing: I want my family home. Linda and Brandon are at school, Megan at day care, and it will be hours before they arrive. The pain of being separated from my daughter for ten days has been massive, impenetrable, and though I know I cannot pick her up for weeks, she can be placed next to me on the couch to snuggle.

I sleep, awaken, remember, doze again.

*

Late in the day, we have already watched a World War II movie, and I feel somewhat better, still weak but not in pain. We have always enjoyed a good film from the war, because Daddy was in it and I am knowledgeable about it. We sometimes talk for hours about tactics, about the Battle of the Bulge, especially about aircraft. (Years later I will have a delightful conversation with William Faulkner's nephew, Jimmy Faulkner, about the Corsairs he flew as a Marine pilot in the South Pacific during World War II and later in Korea.)

Now, though, the thin light of the first day of March is fading, and we are talking about nothing in particular when I hear the rumble of Linda's car and see her parking out front. Something new begins to happen to me now, a lifting of spirits, a stirring of my expectations, and in a moment they are spilling in the door, Brandon first, followed by Linda carrying Megan.

"Daddy!" Megan says.

"Hey," says my wife. "Welcome home."

"Glad you're back," says Brandon.

"Me, too."

"Daddy! Pick me up!" cries Megan.

"I can't, Sweetie," I say. "You climb up here and sit next to me."

"Pick me up!" She realizes I can't, and so she scrambles up on the couch and sits beside me, smiling broadly. She leans to her left into me, and I curl my arm around her, pull her close and kiss her repeatedly on the top of her dark brown hair. Linda leans down and kisses me, and Brandon awkwardly shakes my hand.

"I sure do appreciate you staying with Phil this week," Linda says to my father.

"My pleasure," he says. "We're just watching old movies and so forth."

Soon he's gone, saying he will be there by seven-thirty the next day, which is a Wednesday. Megan brings me a book to read her, and Linda goes to cook dinner while Brandon escapes to his room to play a video game. I realize, startled, that it is indeed all over.

The anxiety of surgery, the descent to the operating room, the examinations, the cutting away of my degenerated valve—all are behind me now. I feel breakable, physically weak, emotionally suspect. But I cannot live past this moment. My sweet daughter is at my side, the smell of chicken begins to rise from the kitchen, and I can hear the sound effects from Brandon's video game. I have returned home to heal, and I believe that my family, that this acreage can restore me.

I believe that I will not see the inside of a hospital again for many years. But we cannot read the future in tea leaves or even our children's eyes. For now, with Megan at my side, I bear the stone of illness lightly. I make peace with my frailties and hold my daughter near my heart.

Blizzard

Weather forecasting has dramatically improved in the past forty years, but in at least one aspect we're still at sea: snow. The vagaries of our southern climate, the swiftness of cold fronts and low-pressure systems, and the often changeable temperatures make predicting snow in north Georgia difficult, if not impossible. Our main criterion is this: If the National Weather Service predicts snow, there won't be any.

I know that our delight with snow and joy at its arrival must seem pure madness to someone in, say, Buffalo. I was in Buffalo in the winter once, and both sides of the street were lined with knee-deep black snow. Ugly. And yet in north Georgia (and in much of the American South), snow has retained its purity.

Even a hint of snow sends schoolchildren (and their parents) out to scan the skies, to see the first unique crystal fall into the trees or eyelashes.

*

I love snow on Wildcat Ridge because it stops the sounds of nature. Slowly, one by one, the winter birds begin to lose their songs. The red-tailed hawks settle down to await developments. The leaf sounds are muffled. Snow also profoundly changes the normal colors here, the slate grays and browns of winter into a shade that is not pastel. The idea that this place is tropical green and dripping in the summer is impossible to consider. Only when the snow has stopped and the ground and trees are laced with chalky ice do the songbirds come back out, usually to great scoops of birdseed that Linda puts out for them.

I can sit for hours in the window of my second-floor library and look out at the woods "filling up with snow." Often, I will listen to Brahms, whom I have come to associate with snow for nostalgic reasons relating to my childhood and the music my parents played. Then I will bundle Megan up and take her outside as I always did Brandon when he was younger.

Those early years in our parenthood, Linda began making snow cats for Brandon, and it became a family tradition. Now, Megan is saying, "Will there be enough snow for a snow cat?"

I tell her I do not know.

*

In the winter of 1993, one year before my surgery, I know. The elements do not conspire, are not sentient, but they are coming for that most unusual weather phenomenon in north Georgia: a blizzard. The weather forecasters on the Atlanta television stations are in full glory, showing the deepening low-pressure system, the massive sieve of water arising from the Gulf of Mexico, and the bitterly cold temperatures in place.

The populace goes wonderfully mad, storming the stores for bread and milk and, in our case, a lot of beer. Nothing worse than being snowbound without beer, though John Greenleaf Whittier failed to mention that in his poem "Snowbound." Maybe he just overlooked it.

In the early morning I am up and have a roaring fire of oak logs in our fieldstone fireplace, and I check the weather radio and the television reports, and no one disagrees this time. In fact, several are using the terms "snowstorm" and "blizzard," something we virtually never face here.

I put on a kids' program for Megan. Linda and Brandon still sleep. I go outside and walk through the edge of the woods looking for signs that the natural world knows what is arriving. A gentle, bitterly cold wind waves the water oak leaves, which will not fall until the last weeks of winter. A leafless poplar waves sturdily, and I look up its gray trunk and see a gray sky.

My face reddens, and I love it. My dogs are standing silent in their pen, looking at me with little motion, and I love it. The fescue lawn is oddly green against the pigeon-colored forest, and I love it.

I come back inside and fumble through my closet, and Linda, half asleep, speaks. "What's it doing out there?"

"Nothing yet. Feels like snow" I say.

"Um. What are you doing in the closet?"

"Getting the video camera. This ought to be good."

"You're going to jinx it." She rolls back over, and before I leave the room she is breathing deeply again. I cannot sleep. I want to see the world change shape and color, to slip even further into its profound silence.

*

I make sure Megan's fine and go back outside, and the wind, calm before, is lifting insistently from the southeast. The air is heavy with water, so heavy I make a cold tunnel through the vapor as I move, or at least it feels that way. I burrow into the heart of winter. I see a cardinal stuck to a pine branch, head turning very slightly, as if to ask me what is happening.

As if. All of nature to a person interested in it is . . . *as if.*

I am certain the cardinal is asking me absolutely nothing, but it's pleasant to think so, and I am no scientist, defend no thesis. I am an interested amateur, and I can bring to bear any conclusion I like without fear of peer pressure or condemnation.

Rain begins. The droplets are hard and almost brittle, sting my face. I snug down my Braves cap just as I notice the rain is flying crazily, that the wind is increasing, waving the treetops in a lovely counterpoint.

I am fascinated with transitions in nature. My friend David Landau, a physicist, studies phase transitions, those points when things change from one state to another. It's a fascinating field and one I do not remotely understand except that it is an elegant way of studying what *is* and what it *will become.* This transition is not subatomic, however, but visible to the naked eye. As I watch, the rain begins to change into sleet.

The sound suddenly changes. The woods and dry leaves are being deluged with rice, or it sounds that way, rice poured straight from a box. The air is splattery, almost sizzling with sleet, and I see a few birds fluff on branches, shaking off the sudden assault of ice. Rain mixes with the ice for a moment, then it fades, and another transition begins. The sleet is now mixed with a softer cousin—snow. And yet this is not a gentle *Nutcracker* kind of snow, falling straight down in enormous clusters of flakes. It is hard and nearly horizontal. I walk to the edge of the forest and see the sleet and snow already starting to stick.

*

Nineteenth-century poets, usually from New England, described these skies as "bleak," but I find them fascinating, because I am a southerner. They are a deep gray, almost smudged with black. Look up into the clouds and you'll see a legion of descending flakes, like angels coming at the Last Judgment in a Hieronymous Bosch painting. Flakes swarm.

I believe they fall irregularly and that no two flakes are alike. And yet I prepare a plan for it, like a short-order cook of nature, pretend at first they are molecules in a vacuum and then bees falling from a hive. I hold my arms and twirl with a middle-aged awkwardness. My God, how I love this!

The light abruptly shifts down in candlepower. The snow increases magnificently. I keep moving, arms up sometimes, down at others, flapping like the Albatross of Wildcat Ridge, ridiculous and not caring. I am the only creature attempting to fly now. The birds have grounded themselves, gone silent. High in a bare tulip poplar a crow sits quietly, head turning ever so slightly in what I choose to think is amazement.

I walk back around the front of the house and notice that the filling has already begun. In the South, snow is a suspicious tenant, melting, coming back, filling, failing. On this day, it has no doubts, so to speak. The clouds are thick and heavy with ice, stretch hundreds of miles back into the Gulf of Mexico.

I put my hands in the pocket of my coat. I cannot fly on the calmest day of spring. I fly only in imagination, which may be the best way. I am lumbering, bundled, grounded, and yet this transition fills me with a calmness and joy.

*

All day the snow falls heavily, blindingly. My family gets up and comes out with me, and we watch the forest turn colors, then go back inside peeling off layers and sit by the fire with coffee or hot chocolate. I cannot stop going to the windows and looking out.

An inch falls, then two, five, seven.

There is nothing left of the gray winter forest. Instead, we are a berg broken off a floe, Arctic-bound, dizzy with amazement at the changes. The pine boughs hang heavy with snow, the cars almost disappear, the birds begin to beg for seeds, which Linda puts out by the bucket load, even though snow covers it up. The birds kick through the piling flakes and find the sunflower seeds, scatter them, send encoded messages to their own kind.

The wind increases to thirty, even forty miles an hour as the snow intensifies throughout the day. I am sitting by the fireplace reading Tennyson when I hear a crack and a crash and run to Megan's bedroom window and look out to see that an oak tree next to the house has crashed into the woods.

"What was that?" Linda asks when I come back.

"Huge tree just blew down," I say. "This is getting ugly."

Throughout the rest of the afternoon, the power flickers from time to time. We live very far into the country, and if the roads are impassible we will not get out of here for a long time. Still, we have milk and bread, plenty of canned goods, and adequate beer and coffee. We can sit it out.

Late afternoon comes, and I become Yuri Zhivago, tramping back from his enforced service with partisans toward Yuriatin. I am a poet, but I am not a man with extraordinary courage. I bundle up for maybe the fifth time and walk up to the road and find that it and the fields have disappeared. Landmarks have vanished. I throw my muffler over my face, just up to the eyes, and walk on the road, pretending that I am heading back for Lara.

Ridiculous, but enjoyable nonetheless. I have told Linda I flapped like a bird in the morning and she warns me not to do it where the neighbors can see.

"Why?" I ask.

"They'll think you're an idiot" is her dry reply, eyes not coming off her book.

I wouldn't mind being considered an idiot, a traveling pilgrim in nineteenth-century Russia.

*

I am deliciously alone. Everything is in motion. I am reduced to my footprints in the muffled snowscape. The wind is sharp, the flakes almost blinding, but I don't try to escape, instead embracing what could kill me in a few hours of exposure.

Southerners, to use Robert Frost's poem as a reference point, always believe they will die in fire, not ice. I do not want to die in either, but I follow my visible breath on a long walk before I turn, head back home.

*

Late in the afternoon the power goes out. Considering the blizzard whistling outside, we suspect it could be hours, if not days, before it comes back on, and so I set about sealing off the great room with our fieldstone fireplace. I hang blankets over the open doorways, stoke up the fire, make sure we have plenty of wood on the porch. The house grows cold rather too quickly for my taste, and we are soon huddled around the fire, wearing layers of clothing, coats and hats. The indoor temperature plummets to around fifty degrees and holds. We eat cold cuts for supper, and I take some of the food from the fridge and put it on the frigid back porch.

How odd in this kingdom of algae and fungi! We light candles against the cold darkness, which comes very soon. I keep thinking the power from our rural electric corporation will be restored soon, but I'm wrong. No need to try calling. The phone's dead, too. We try to read a little by firelight, give it up and go to our respective beds, huddled up in rooms far colder than the great room. All night I get up every forty minutes or so and feed the fire. I sleep only a little and do not mind the wakefulness as much as the cold.

*

By late the next afternoon the power is still off. The house is bitterly cold. We have saved enough water to flush the toilets, but that's about it. The storm has moved up the East Coast, leaving us with downed trees and nine inches of snow, a foot or more in the drifts. People in the Northeast would find our reaction to such an amount of snow laughable, but we are unprepared, seldom see a blizzard. I go outside several times during the morning, and Wildcat Ridge is magnificent. I cook breakfast on our grill on the snowy back porch.

By late in the day we are crabby, tired, cold. The sun has not come out, so the house, even with candles, is very dark, and it is too hard to read—the only real disaster of the storm so far. We have no idea what will happen next, and even with the fire roaring the room is cold and the rest of the house is unspeakable. Linda feeds the birds all day long, speaks softly to them. They come in enormous flocks, everything from cardinals and chickadees to messy, noisy blue jays. I read for a while, go back to the windows inevitably, unable to stay away from the frozen world.

Like a heart being restarted after surgery, the power suddenly flickers around six in the evening, goes off, then comes back on and stays on.

"Hallelujah!" we cry. We wait for a few minutes as the house begins to heat, and then I triumphantly pull down the blankets that have hung over the open doorways. Within an hour, we're back to seventy degrees, and we have regained communications with the world. We will remain snowbound for nearly a week, but we'll do it with power and heat.

After dark I go outside and find that the stars have come out and that the snow looks clean and pure, enveloping. The ice-crafted images before me are lovely and unrecognizable. I feel a longing in my bones for the steppes, for small fireplaces burning peat, for comfort in another tongue.

Two Weeks

I spend the first week home from the hospital in misery. I have always slept on my side, but I cannot do it now because of my incision and the drainage bag. I exercise by walking around the sofas in our den, but I do not go outside. The idea of climbing the stairs to my study is laughable; I barely have the strength to move from one room to another. Nights are the worst. I awaken in cold sweats, hear the valve ticking in my chest, wonder how I can ever bear this. My only salvation is family.

My father comes over every morning, bringing old movies on videotapes. We go through World War II and one day watch *The Quiet Man*, probably one of John Wayne's best movies. I awaken, take my medicine, take naps, walk around furniture. I get no stronger.

*

Daddy and I have been talking about Normandy when the pain in my shoulder begins. Though I have talked to the doctor, and he says not to worry, these sieges terrify me, because when you are fragile, any pain is amplified a hundredfold.

"It's happening again," I groan. At first, it's like a heaviness, but then the pain assaults me in the back of the shoulder and just down my left arm, and I realize I am groaning, crying out.

"Do you want me to rub it?" he asks.

"Yes," I gasp.

My father is sitting beside me on the sofa, and he reaches around me and begins to rub the spot, and I begin to cry. I am not ashamed. He takes me in his arms and rubs my back as I rest my head on his shoulder. The pain grows monstrous. I want to scream, to curse, but I grimly hang on and choke back my tears, try to fight it with fierce determination. Finally, after five or six minutes of ghastly suffering, the pain begins to ease, and then, with a sudden relaxation, it's gone.

"Okay," I gasp. "It's gone now."

"Sure?"

"Yeah."

He gets up and goes back to his sofa, and it occurs to me that the pain came on and left precisely like a cramp—that in fact the doctor is right about this being displaced thoracic pain. Mentally, I feel somewhat better, though my weakness is a drug to which I will never become addicted.

I was surprised to find myself in my father's arms. A man expects certain things in life never to happen again. As I said before, I knew when Brandon was about nine that I would soon never hold his hand again when crossing a street, and so I carefully watched each time it happened. The last time was crossing Lumpkin Street on the way to his cello lesson in Athens.

On these early spring days I wish I were crossing Wildcat Ridge. I wish I were a whole man, and that I could drive to the grocery store, read books, dig a hole. I wish I were crossing Wildcat Ridge from one end to the other, looking down at the creek and exulting in that historic flow. I wish I were crossing Wildcat Ridge because it might convince me that I will live forever, as I thought when I was a child.

I would give my kingdom to be crossing Wildcat Ridge.

*

As scheduled, I go to the ER, and they remove the drainage bag after a week, and good riddance. Every day my father and I watch movies, listen to classical music, eat a light lunch, take naps. After lunch I go back to the bedroom and lie down. Some days I sleep for two or three hours. On the fifth day home, I walk around both sofas twice.

On the weekend my family gathers around me, and I manage to push myself a bit: to walk farther, to sit on the porch and look at the natural world around us. Brandon is full of news about school and video games, about his friends. His life is rich, beginning. I envy him with love, because I remember being that age quite clearly. I was just realizing that my life was to be one of creativity, and I would paint, write, and compose constantly, blissfully unaware of what was good or bad. I have often thought that the great gift of the arty adolescence is the need to create without the critical sense to worry about quality.

How I wish I could retrieve that feeling as I work! But that innocence, like all other kinds, is lost. During this recovery, however, the idea of work is an alien thing, like a huge boulder one is told to move with a shoulder.

*

The second week after surgery I am feeling somewhat stronger than when I first came home, and the shoulder cramps come less often and with less severity. My father still comes for me, and we follow the same patterns we have for more than four decades, though I don't have enough strength to argue politics, something we have always enjoyed.

One sunny day I walk a bit around the front yard, shuffling in my bedroom slippers and cotton exercise pants. There is clear evidence of spring, and I want to feel that resurrection in my veins, but it eludes me. No matter. I walk farther than I have yet, and I am beginning to become accustomed to things.

A good example is the ticking in my chest. One night, lying awake long after Linda has fallen asleep beside me, the ticking is audible, and it feels horrible, Poe-esque, and I believe I may go mad. I ball my hands into fists. Then, in imagination, I am standing in my grandmother's house, in her living room, and I am alone and looking at the clock on her mantel, and it is ticking with the same sound in my chest. I immediately fall into a heavy, dreamless sleep, and when I awaken I know that this ticking is now a comfort, not a fear, because I always felt loved in my grandmother's house. From that day onward the sound is my sinecure, my haven, my constant and salving companion.

*

On Friday, March 11, 1994, I am feeling better than I have since I came home, stronger, surer that I will survive this experience, which has been harrowing. When I hear men shrug off open-heart surgery with macho bravado, I know they're lying. Not that men lying about their feelings is anything unusual. Most men would rather be dead than admit they ever *had* a feeling.

My father has served his time with me. The following week I'll go solo, because I can take care of myself now reasonably well. I'll watch TV, read a little, practice walking outside in the yard. I try to express my gratitude, but Daddy refuses to accept my thanks for precisely the right reason: Love requires no thanks. In a world of ghastly, broken families, I am blessed among all men to have had a mother and father who are loving, endlessly interested in the world, and who treated me with pride when I first began to write poetry.

The world is a brighter place that Friday, and I spend the day with my family, enjoying the small increments of life and affections, the small arguments, the unexpected laughter.

That night I actually read in bed for a while, not the heavy Troyat biography of Tolstoy but a thick paperback, the Carlos Baker biography of Hemingway, long a favorite, a book I've read several times already. I read until I'm drowsy, tell my wife good night, and close my eyes, slipping straight into sleep.

Sometime in the night I awaken feeling strange, and I decide to go to the bathroom, but as soon as I sit on the edge of the bed, I know something is terribly wrong. My left side doesn't appear to be attached to me any longer. I think I must be dreaming, and so I stand and begin to walk to the bathroom, and I am stumbling, falling, twisting, not feeling my left foot at all. I try to catch the doorknob into the bathroom, but my left hand has no feeling, and I reach to the floor just beside the tub.

"Linda! Help me!" I hear my voice saying. I repeat it over and over, and she stumbles sleepily to me, turns on the light.

"What's wrong? Did you fall?"

"I can't feel my left side at all. You'd better call the doctor."

"Are you all right?"

"Just call the doctor."

"Okay."

I know what is happening, and the fear comes back.

Spring

*The jonquils have long since risen from the shadows. Fair-
weather cumulus clouds puff up on a western wind, mark a
transit down Wildcat Creek. A rustling. New green in the
undercanopy, dogwoods spreading white petals, native
azaleas pink and purple falling down the steep hill toward
water. A sense of motion comes in the morning, of wings and
new growth, and creatures moving in the earth. The sun-
warmed pine needles shudder. A turkey hen nabs bugs in the
meadow. The late-day sun hangs a few minutes longer,
throwing sharp highlights along the threads of a garden
spider's web, and shadows from leaves begin to spill across
the forest floor. Spring is not the season of hope, just another
angling of mass away from the sun. The stack of firewood:
growing no smaller. The venerable ridge: sliding down by
centuries.*

Wildflowers

In early March the trilliums pop up through the loamy soil of the woods behind our house, where the land slopes sharply down to Wildcat Creek. Though they flourish north of here, we have plenty, and each year this forest fills itself with mottled green leaves at the end of a straight fuse, surmounted by a lovely, dark purple flower.

Our variety, I think, is the sessile trillium (*Trillium cuneatum*), which is not uncommon in rich forest soils. Some of the other varieties are quite rare. The simple trillium (without an adjective) has flowers that smell like lemons, though they don't grow here. There are sixteen species of trilliums in all, from the Rose to the Painted. All love rich forest soil and are perennial.

The sessile trilliums are painted in their hundreds down the slope. The flowers are a deep, rich purple that is only a few shades from brown. Similar species can be very rare, but ours is abundant, even common, though that word describes the flower's presence, not its beauty. Of all the wildflowers on Wildcat Ridge, the trilliums are the most abundant, though they are gone by early May. They are bookmarks for the season, a promise that more sunlight is beginning to saturate the spaces between the oak and hickory forest.

*

If we have trillions of trilliums in the early spring, the real season of wildflowers in the South is high summer. On our seven acres alone we have identified the common morning glory, oxeye daisies, ruella, daisy fleabane, puccoon, bull nettle, passionflower, sickle-pod, narrow-leaved sunflower, Florida violet, three-lobed violet, Queen Anne's lace, angelica, bitterweed, rough sunflower, and musk thistle, among many flowers that grow either in the woods or sun. We are still identifying species, and even with Wilbur Duncan's magnificent *Wildflowers of the Southeastern United States*, identification comes slowly.

Today it's hot, and the day has almost evaporated into the west. I'm sitting on the edge of our dirt road, staring at a small yellow flower and flipping pages madly, trying to find *anything* that resembles the small corolla and bracts. Linda, who doesn't like to sit in the dirt or grass, is leaning over me, looking down at the book.

"That's it," I say, finger on a color plate.

"No, the leaves are wrong," she says. "See?"

"Oh, yeah."

She's right, of course, which frustrates me, but some wildflowers resist taxonomy, and some days identifying them is like herding cats.

Megan comes up bearing a small fistful of something purple. "Daddy, look what I found!" she says. "What are they called?"

I look at them, have no idea, and take them from her for later study. She doesn't seem to care that I've failed, for I don't sell myself as an expert, just as one interested enough to jump into the rainbow of local flowers and identify my way out.

The most beautiful and exotic flower we have is the passionflower (*Passiflora incarnata*), which also goes by the prosaic name of maypop. It's a trailing perennial with spectacularly fringed purple petals and loves roadside or thin woods. Trilliums and passionflowers don't seek the same ground. When it turns yellow, the pulpy fruit of the passionflower (the maypop) is edible, but I've never tried one.

*

Sickle-pod and musk thistles have lovely flowers, the former a delicate yellow, the latter a brazen pink. Don't tell farmers these plants have any redeeming qualities, though, because they see them merely as weeds. And each is a formidable enemy, especially the musk thistle, which is especially prevalent around here.

I spent seven years as a science writer for the University of Georgia College of Agriculture, and in that time I visited dozens of farms, as well as our own test plots, and nothing brought a quicker scowl than incipient sickle-pod, which seemed to lurk at the fringes of a field and then leap, en masse, into the rows. In the late 1970s scientists found that sickle-pod was poisonous "when eaten in considerable amounts," referring, I suppose, to cattle, since I can't imagine a human grazing on this common plant. We do know it can host the tobacco etch virus, which can destroy crop plants.

The musk thistles can be more than three feet tall, and they seed by wind dispersal around here beginning in mid-June or so.

*

Megan loves the little Florida violets, which grow in profusion in shady places behind our house. I have on occasion cut them back from paths with my lawn mower, and it makes no difference to the violets, which spring right back and keep on spreading. Their scientific name is elegant: *Viola floridana*.

Some wildflowers are so small, so subtle, that you can miss them without strict attention to your field of vision. Others, like common bitterweed, are so pervasive as to be nearly invisible—we tend to screen out what we see every day. And yet bitterweed, which cattle notoriously avoid, has a vivid, pungent odor and a pretty yellow flower.

Queen Anne's lace and angelica are my favorite white flowers. The carrots we eat are related to Queen Anne's lace, and you can actually eat the young roots of Queen Anne's lace, which bears the somewhat uncommon alternate name of wild carrot. I tasted one once, but it was bitter, nothing I'd expect to find in a salad bar. Some folks also think Queen Anne's lace is a weed, but I love everything about it, from its species name (*Daucus carota*) to its round white flowers. Angelica resembles small Queen Anne's lace, though it flowers in clusters rather than singly. Wildlife experts once thought angelica was poisonous, but that seems to have been a canard.

The interested amateur can approach the world from any point he wishes.

*

Most of our wildflowers are the species that love shade, since we largely live in the forest, but we border on sunlight in many open places, and sun lovers take up residence here quickly. I cannot imagine how many species we will ultimately identify, but there are a great many I cannot find in any of my books, and asking an expert for help seems like cheating. Maybe we will make up names for some of them. Or perhaps I will rename them all into my own familial taxonomy.

We could have Megan's lavender, Wildcat clover, Philip's crested dwarf-root, Linda-pod, or Brandon madder. The Meggie glory (*Ipomoea purpurea megana*) and the narrow-lobed Williams vetch. The Linda's slipper. Oconee three-tongued bladderwort.

*

I carry Megan's purple flowers with me, and I still don't know what they are. If I don't find out, she won't care.

It's July now, a long time from March, but already I can imagine the purple flowers of trilliums opening in the deep woods. They are not the end of a cycle or a beginning—just a point at which we humans, who bloom all too early, can mark the forward motion of our years.

Back in the Hospital

I am lying on the bathroom floor, and slowly feeling is coming back to my left side. I work my hand and lift my foot. Linda has dialed the cardiologist, and he's on the phone, which she brings to me.

"I'm getting better," I say. "I can feel things again."

"Just talk to him."

The cardiologist on call is not my regular doctor, and it's clear I've awakened him, as he listens to my symptoms. My voice probably betrays my fright.

"Why don't you go on to the emergency room and let's get this checked out?" he says.

"Okay." I hang up and hand the phone to Linda, gather myself to a sitting position by the tub, and then stand. There's still a tingling, but the numbness that lasted for perhaps six or seven minutes after I awakened is gone. Perhaps I rolled oddly to my side and the arm and leg "went to sleep." But more worrisome is the possibility of a TIA—a transient ischemic attack, what are popularly called "little strokes."

In the early post-operative stages of heart-valve replacement these can happen, though they are the exception. They may not be a serious problem and may result from blood-borne "debris" from the surgery that reaches the brain. On the other hand, they could mean my Coumadin level is insufficient and that blood clots are forming on my valve.

Linda gets Brandon up, and he comes down to sleep on the couch so he will be near Megan through the night. We trust him to look out after her for a few hours. I dress in my same old exercise pants, and soon we're in the car and Linda's driving through the night. It is about one o'clock and I feel tired and sick at heart. I keep flexing my hand, raising my foot, flexing my hand, raising my foot, and by now I feel all right, but I am deeply unhappy at revisiting the hospital a bare two weeks after my dismissal.

"You all right?" Linda asks, as always the soul of calmness.

"I think so," I say. "I just woke up, and it was like my left side wasn't there. Pretty weird."

"What do you think it was?"

"Find something on the radio."

She gets a talk show from Chicago, one of her staples, and I hear syllables, consonants and vowels, but I cannot translate them into words. They slide past me, a foreign language.

*

The emergency room of Athens Regional has the soft, strange lighting of an Edward Hopper painting. A few people are in the waiting area as we come in, painted there, it seems. We go through the admissions drill, and soon enough they are taking me back into a curtained cubicle, where a pleasant ER nurse gets vital signs and fills out a clipboard sheet. The light is all fluorescent, therefore unreal. I dislike fluorescent light, which to me turns everything into a ghastly pale German expressionist color, but I don't hold it against the hospital, which, after all, is the place where doctors saved my life.

I lie flat on my back, reasonably calm, while Linda sits in the corner reading a paperback book she has cannily brought. I am thinking of nothing in particular when the curtain opens and an impossibly young doctor comes walking in. He squeezes my foot, and the human contact immediately relaxes me.

"What we got here?" he asks, reading from the clipboard. "Numbness on the left side, post-valve surgery?" We shake hands, and he begins the standard neurological tests, and I feel everything, respond normally when prompted. This takes some time, and I answer his questions sharply and briefly, often in single syllables.

"Got any ideas?" I ask finally.

"Well, it could be a TIA—that's what we'd worry about in a situation like this, but there doesn't seem to have been any lasting damage," he says. "We'll get a CAT scan and see what that tells us."

"And if there's no sign of a problem there?"

He raises his hand to me and rapidly folds his fingers down three times in succession—an unexpected signal for good-bye—for dismissal. I feel better knowing this, but I feel worse when a few minutes later they roll me back through the ER's communications center toward the CAT scan room.

*

I thought I was through with all this. But, like a recurring nightmare, I'm back in the innards of the hospital, ready to be inserted into a magnificent machine whose inventor won the Nobel Prize. Before, they wanted to look at my heart, but now my brain is the point of concern. If there are signs of bleeding, I may have had a stroke. The technician on the night shift seems absolutely glad to have some business, and I try to be as relaxed and chatty as possible, though I'm sleepy and want to go home to my children.

"This won't take long," he says.

"Good," I say. "Unfortunately I have plenty of time. I'm home recuperating from valve surgery. Had some numbness."

"They think a TIA or what?"

"Could be, but I don't think so."

Actually, I do think so, but the age-old desire to wish away illness has entered me strongly in the past few days. I can't wish away the ticking in my chest, but perhaps I can wish my brain into a normal state. The tests do not take long, and soon I'm being rolled back to the emergency room, where I wait and wait and Linda reads.

Finally, the doctor comes back, and he doesn't look too concerned, either. For all I know, he's been working a car wreck or a gunshot the last hour.

"Well, the CAT scan was good, no problems there, but I talked to your doctor, and he thinks we ought to go ahead and admit you so we can adjust your Coumadin level and make sure everything's all right. Get you on heparin for a few days and get you regulated, maybe on the high side a bit. You'll be fine."

"If I'm fine, why do I have to go back in the hospital?"

"Your doctor thinks it's the right thing to do," he says.

I have never mistrusted my medical advice, and I'm not about to start now. I nod. Linda is standing beside me. "How long will he have to stay in?" she asks.

"Hard to say. Up to your doctor, but probably no more than a few days, I'd think. The nurse will be back when they have a room available."

We shake hands, and he's gone. I put my left palm over my eyes and shake my head. Linda reassures me with her calm, steady voice and goes back to her paperback. I lie back and watch the clock on the wall as it ticks uselessly around the numbers.

*

It's just after 5:30 before I'm admitted and taken upstairs to a private room, and the feeling of the elevator rising beneath me is familiar and disturbing. I thought it would be years before I was back in this position, and it has been two weeks. We get to the fourth floor, and a nurse at the station sees me coming through. "Are you back?" she asks.

"I'm afraid so," I answer. "Some numbness. Might have been nothing, but they want me back in to make sure."

"I'm sorry," she says. "Let us know if you need anything."

Within five minutes, I'm in the bed and Linda is getting ready to head home to get the children ready for the day, which is a Saturday. No doubt she's exhausted, but she won't admit it, because she doesn't wear her feelings openly as I do.

"I'll come back later this morning, and if you need anything, give me a call," she says. "Do you want me to call people?"

"I'll call my parents," I say. "You can call anybody else if you think they need to know."

"I will." She kisses me on the cheek and is gone.

*

Time lies heavily on me. I doze, awaken, feel a deep and growing depression, like a monstrous tumor that may be large enough to take over the world. Was it really a stroke or a TIA? If the valve is "throwing clots," will I have a heart attack? I am still weak from the surgery, and now the glimmer of hope for my health seems to have slipped from me.

Or perhaps I simply rolled awkwardly to my left side in sleep, and my arms and legs, folded beneath me, "went to sleep." (My new admission record, which I will not see until several years later, says: "Transient Ischemic Attack Status Post Mitral Valve Replacement." That word *status* means that such an attack was possible and I was being treated as if it happened, though a diagnosis was not certain.) Whatever happened, I am back in the hospital. If my heart is healing, if my sternum is starting to grow back together, if there is no evidence of intercranial bleeding, then my mind is clearly suffering. After years of living near the edge of my feelings, I am being paid back.

I hold the sheets with both my hands and begin to sweat. I have never been one to operate on the dubious strength of my body but on the scope of memory and knowledge. I have read thousands of books and retained important parts. I have been burdened with aspirations and have achieved a minor sort of success as a novelist, poet, and journalist. And yet there is much more I want to do, and none of it revolves around literature or music or art. It involves my wife and kids, my parents, my sister Laura Jane and her family, my brother Mark and his.

I want life, not art—steady, enduring sanity. Not *this*.

I want this terrible city of illness to fade in my rearview mirror. I want to be whole and walking on my land, on any land, feeling the assurances of childhood. I do not want to do what I begin doing as the sunrise breaks. I do not want to cry.

Shadows

Seasons change, years pass. The winter sun hangs low, yawns, never gets up very far. In high summer the heat is blistering, the light strong and urgent. All year, even on the nights of moon, our land lives in shadows.

When Brandon was very small, he discovered his own shadow in our driveway and tried to extricate himself from it, lifting one foot, then the other, and finally running inside to escape the clinging beast. I had to explain that his shadow was not a bad thing, but he wanted rid of it as much as Peter Pan wanted his back.

The natural world runs on shade and shadow like a car runs on gasoline, but we consider shadows very little. Since my family and I live in the woods, light comes in patches, except in the cleared area around the house, and the rest of our seven acres are in a duller light that sometimes seems lustrous.

We live in those shadows and swim in the mottled light.

*

Fire ants don't live in the shade. For reasons not really understood, they require direct sunlight. Just so, many creatures live at the edge of the woods or in fields where the light is strong. Hawks usually hunt in fields where the light is good and the line of sight is vast.

And yet our north Georgia forests bask in their layered shadows. The overcanopy of oaks and sweet gums and hickories shades the understory of native azalea, persimmon, and dozens of small bushes. Dozens of birds live in the first story, while thousands of species of insects reside beneath the lowest story of shade. Certain tunnel spiders weave in our front porch boxwoods, while others remain in the recesses of the woods. Fungi love the deep shade, especially down along the creek, where they grow in slimy glory along rotten deadfall.

*

It is peculiar how people react to light. Most would choose bright sun over a cloudy day anytime. They would choose warmth over cold, eschew shadow. There is even a condition called Seasonal Affective Disorder to describe those unable to tolerate long, gray winters. Travel literature is full of stories about heading for the tropics. Northerners constantly daydream about getting out of Detroit and heading to Miami Beach.

I choose shadows and autumn.

Mark and I grew up in the woods in Morgan County, spending whole weekends there as boys, exploring and pretending. In the woods, I could be Lewis and he could be Clark. A pile of rocks would be a suitable Troy. We camped in the pine forest behind our house, listened to the night sounds around a campfire, slept in our War Surplus jungle hammocks as rain pelted us.

He lives in woods now, too. Once you are deeply attached to forest and shadow, you can never really live in a town. Our parents have found this somewhat peculiar because our life in the country was only a relatively short interlude for them, from 1953 to 1961. But for us, it was our childhood.

I still admire a fine pasture, an open field, and the sight of a hunting raptor can reduce me to stillness for an hour or more. But in the country around these parts, forest is the most common sight.

*

Today it's early spring and the leaves have greened. I am walking around in the woods, where the undercanopy has not yet popped out into green. During the winter our forest is a slate gray, matching the color of the house. I stand on a cluster of boulders and reach out from shadow into the sun. The sunlight warms my hand slightly, warmth that then fades when I pull it back.

If my lumbering body can feel that difference, imagine what cities of insects can feel. If my eyes know it, how do the eyes of a raccoon react?

I walk slowly down the paths I have cut. Some are in fine shape, while others, less used, are being crowded by growth from the summer before. All around me, the shadows are coming back. They swirl around the treetops, slide down the thick gray trunks, fall to the ground, a dizzy dappling.

We all enjoy early spring, though it means less here than in the colder climates where it presages something like salvation. Here, spring is no epiphany, just a gentle reawakening. When leaves come back, shadows come back, too. I try to understand their taxonomy, but it's vague, in poor order. Leaf shadows swirl, spread a mottled light from bush to forest floor. As the sun climbs, the angle changes and shadows move. I am a shadow chaser, and today the leaves cast flowing patches of darkness around me.

*

I also find pleasure in moonshadows. When the pale yellow chalk-ball of moon is full, the tree shadows, especially in winter, are dazzling. But our house has its shadow, as does my old truck and the well house. Our bluebird feeders cast shadows.

My own moonshadow is a cool companion, a silent partner in the world of owl cries. Sometimes I conduct invisible orchestras in moonshadow and watch my arms rise and fall, build to the impossible climax of Mahler's *Symphony No. Eight*. Once when I was conducting in the moonlight, I saw a neighbor dog standing on his own shadow not twenty feet away, staring silently, amazed.

The shadow of a swooping screech owl on a moony night is almost impossible to see, because the eye follows the majestic raptor, but I did it once out of dumb stubbornness, and it was no more than a quick leaf-fall, a small flutter on the grass.

*

The hardest shadows to study are the ones cast by an over-canopy on tree trunks, or the delicate shadow put down by a slender sprig of grass. In most situations, we tend to see shadows as color shifts, and that is especially true in hardwood forests, where everything much of the year revolves around two colors: green and gray. And yet there are thousands of shades of those two colors. Do the cardinals go for a certain shade of green the way hummingbirds seek the color red?

(Once, when I was wearing a University of Georgia Bulldog T-shirt, a female hummingbird tried valiantly to find where she could sip pollen off me, coming up time after time in a sudden whirr and then appearing confused about where to begin. I sat as still as possible, and the confused creature came back seven or eight time befores giving it up.)

Most animals aren't like fire ants or hunting hawks; they don't love the full sun all the time. They want at least a partial umbrella from the summer heat of Georgia. Some live under rocks and rarely come out. Our deer use the trees not for shadow but for cover. Knowing us as suckers, they graze in our open spots like placid cows, not even running off when they see us out walking. Only when we come very close will they retreat into the sinecure of forest.

*

I have seen alley-shadows from midnight buildings in Manhattan and found them exciting, but I have always been heading back toward the childhood shadows of long pines, of the silence and the stillness that a man alone can find.

You still see old people sitting on porches in the country evenings, rocking or fanning themselves, sipping a sweating glass of sweet tea. They have retreated into the shadows of both age and the hour, and I want to be like that some day, a placid old man with a long white beard. I want to rock in the shadows of my porch and ancestry. I will huddle my grandchildren around me and tell of the great shadows of Wildcat Ridge, and how once I was a full-sized man and stood at night watching the moon swing shades of gray and green and black around me, orchestrating a great opera of subtle voices.

I will tell them of my childhood, of the placid and woodsy 1950s, when I went into the deep forest alone at the age of seven and spent all day in the company of imaginary Indians and real shadows. I will use my spotted hands to draw light pictures on the summer air. I will tell them of the time I saw the shadow of an owl sweep across the earth before me, and I knew that I was likely the only person on the planet at that moment deliberately pulling an owl's shadow over him like a cloak.

I will let them think I am an old fool. I probably will be an old fool. I will pass on to them the guardianship of my memories and the soft, enduring world of shadows.

A Late Spring

Back in this magnificent isolation, I pull up the thin blanket, careful not to brush the IV in the back of my hand. This time, there are no visitors. I call my parents, all but lie about the reason I have returned. I claim probable awkwardness in bed, one side numb from slumping to port in my dreams. I do not believe it. Far more likely is a blood clot that passed into my brain. Perhaps another will come. For more than an hour I have imagined myself into the highways of vasculature, from the aortic freeways to small-town capillary lanes. Or perhaps they are rivers and streams, the Danube and Wildcat Creek, pouring through me on a red tide. To a post-operative clot, each is navigable and leads to the city of the brain.

I have been taking a drug called sodium warfarin, better known by its trade name Coumadin. Its job, as I have said, is to prevent the clumping of platelets into clots, but if there has been a failure, I fear it is mine. Now, the IV drips heparin, the bigger brother of Coumadin, into my bloodstream, and I still doubt it can stop the clots as they form in the blood.

*

How does it come, death? For the length of my ordeal, death has been my silent partner, a body-companion, whistling and playing solitaire, humming the *dies irae* with genial persistence. I have feared him more than ever before. And yet he seems in no special hurry, content to nudge me with a bony finger, in no rush for a full embrace. But more now, I fear madness. That kingdom coats me like a frost. I am not sure I can bear the ticking in my heart, the pooling threat of clots that may journey to the Patagonias of anatomy and rush back to jam the beating heart.

Even worse is the fear of full cerebral vascular "accident," as doctors idiotically call a stroke. I can imagine my eternal sleep well enough, but I cannot bear the dream of my brain's twilight. If illness is another country, stroke is another galaxy.

*

Nurses shuttle to me, then away, like worker ants. Dr. Sinyard, the genial colleague of Dr. Magill, is on call for the weekend, and he tells me it could have been a TIA, but perhaps it wasn't. The idea now is to "thin" my blood a bit more in case my valve did "throw" a platelet clot.

"How long will I have to be here?" I ask. The IV suddenly hurts my hand, but I don't touch it.

"Couple or three days, I'd say," he answers. "Just have to see, but I'm sure you'll be fine. Sometimes it takes a while for the body to adjust to having an artificial valve, but it will. You'll be back to your regular life before you know it."

"I hope so. What about, uh, the emotional aspects?"

He tells me that depression is not uncommon after heart surgery and that people sometimes need counseling or medicines to help. Dr. Magill can tell me more about that when he comes to check me Monday morning. I thank him, watch television for a while, look out the window at a world that keeps moving on wheels and feet.

*

Linda comes to visit me, cheerful and newsy, and I want to put on a disguise and flee with her.

"We could get out during the shift-change for the nurses," I say.

"As fast as you're moving these days, you wouldn't make it to the elevator," she says with studied nonchalance. She's right. I'm a ghost here, a slow-moving shade with the tenuous steps of a very old man.

*

I sleep fitfully Saturday night, endure Sunday. I don't make calls to tell people I'm back in the hospital because I'd be home before they could come to visit. I do not read. I drum my fingers on the sheets or my cheek and think of healing and sacrifice. I have always worried about dying young, but it was an abstract proposition, one of those imaginary tragedies we brew to collect undue pity. Now, my youth is largely gone, and I fear dying in middle age. I begin to consider old age for the first time and discover that I covet that image of the white-bearded sage, an old fellow with a sweet temperament and kind memories. I want to peel off calendar leaves, redraw Megan's height with a pencil up the kitchen wall.

*

I do not want to walk, but I do it anyway, pushing my medicine stand with its bag of heparin down the hall. I am still very weak, but not with the throbbing uncertain steps of the postoperative.

My two weeks at home seem like a cruel dream. For the first time I begin to know how they feel, those who come to the hospital for the last time. And yet I am still looking for the trail out of here. I want to round a sofa and find myself from twenty years before, just starting out as a journalist and a poet. I want to warn the optimistic young man that middle age is a shoals and to beware. But I merely mumble hellos. Quite unexpectedly, I run into my boss from the University of Georgia, Don Eastman, and his wife, Chris. They have come to be with their son who has had surgery.

"I thought you were out," Don says.

"I was," I say. "Then I came back."

"You okay?"

"Oh yeah. Just a thing about getting my medicine balanced. I'll be out in a few days."

"You hang in there."

"Y'all do, too."

*

During this stay they're giving me heparin, Xanax, Lanoxin, Tenormin, Quiniglute, Coumadin, Darvocet, baby aspirin, Persantine, Dalmane, Alparazolam, digoxin, atenelol, dipyridamole, warfarin, and flurazepam. I have yet another echocardiogram and my "mitral prosthesis" is in place and apparently has "good leaflet motion."

I have mild anemia, but that's due to the post-operative course of recovery, the doctors think. The technicians from the blood lab bleed me several times.

*

On Monday afternoon they take me off heparin, and Dr. Magill tells me that I can go home the following day. I am pleased and worried. "It's possible it was a TIA, but we can't say for sure," he says. "But you seem to be doing fine now. I think you'll go on and recover on schedule at home."

I thank him, hesitate, tell him I need to talk about something else. He doesn't rush me. He listens with his eyes and ears. I start to explain that as a writer I have kept my nerves flayed for years, like dipping into a vein for gold. He nods.

"To be honest with you, I feel like I'm losing my mind," I say. "Probably not the right clinical term."

"This happens a good deal after heart surgery," he says. "But they have wonderful medicines now. Would you like for me to recommend you to a psychiatrist?"

I am stunned to find myself nodding, and he tells me about Dr. Thomas Windall (not his real name), who he is sure can help me. He also writes me a prescription for Ativan, which I had been taking before surgery.

"I just go see Dr. Windall?" I ask.

"We'll make the appointment. You'll like him."

I feel grateful and want to know if I will ever again feel normal, but I don't ask and send Dr. Magill off with a quiet thank-you.

*

My father comes back for me on Tuesday morning. My discharge instructions include the following: *Activity—as tolerated—no heavy lifting.* I find this grimly hilarious as I can barely hold the Tolstoy biography yet. I have an appointment with Dr. Magill on April 14 and with Dr. Windall in one week, on March 22.

My discharge nurse, Kristen, has beautiful handwriting, but my own signature is nearly illegible.

"Any questions?" she asks.

"Yeah, can I walk out this time?" I ask. I try on a smile like someone trying on a shirt that no longer fits.

"Transportation will be up," she says, with her own nice smile.

It takes decades for Transportation to come, light years, and this time even the thin patina of victory has evaporated for me. I don't say much of anything as a young man pushes me to the elevator and down, back to the kingdom of the well.

*

My father will stay through Friday, then I am determined to recuperate on my own. I will drive again. I will walk outside in the greening world. I will aim for resurrection of my body and mind, and I will try to make new pacts with those I love. I want to feel strong and calm and centered. I want to walk on Wildcat Ridge and learn my place in this lovely land. I want to write new books, understand *anything* about Wittgenstein, listen to Bach with old ears and new insights. I want to see Brandon go to college and become the scholar I think he is meant to be. I want Megan to grow through slow summers, her brown hair long and swaying, the dark eyes full of mischief.

I want my mind whole. I do not wish to be the victim of family myths, of genetic tragedies.

We drive out of Athens south toward Oconee County, and

this time I don't have shoulder cramps or feel any hint of victories to come. My father plays something on his tape deck—Mozart?—that fails to stick.

The pastures are greening. I flex my hands for the exercise. In one week, it will be the vernal equinox—spring.

Fireflies

In late spring the forest lights up, and those lights remain shining until fall. In May I keep a close eye out for the first sign of my favorite beetle: the lightning bug. Is there anybody who doesn't enjoy the delicate glow of these creatures? They are supposed to flourish near open woods and meadows, but I've seen them in almost every place imaginable.

This is the family *Lampyridae*, and I have a hard time distinguishing the two common species, the Pyralis firefly (*Photinus pyralis*) and the Pennsylvania firefly (*Photuris pennsylvanicus.*) The main difference seems to be that the head of the *Pyralis* is visible from above while that of the Pennsylvania isn't and the light of the latter is more green than yellow. I have read that the flash patterns are different, too. I think most of "my" fireflies are *Pyralis*.

I adore that green-yellow light, which they flash to attract and identify mates. Since most adults apparently don't eat, attracting a mate is about their only job.

*

Few memories of childhood are sweeter than playing outside near dusk in summer, a long day of pleasure in the woods and fields ending with the creak of an ice-cream freezer or one last attempt to see an ever-fainter baseball flying toward me. Those evenings in my memory are always spotted with lightning bugs, and I recall running after them, feeling myself lift as they lilted on light and wings. I did not know then that the only ones flying are the males, since the females are flightless, though they also flash their lights.

I knew that fireflies were the rising cream of a summer evening, however. I can imagine our species evolving together, for if we feel such delight in these beetles, I am certain that earlier peoples did as well. I do not know of any traditions from American Indians regarding lightning bugs, but surely these creatures must fit somewhere in varied spirit tales.

That isn't to say I don't build fancies around the flight of fireflies. I do. I try to choreograph them with my eyes, a Balanchine of the north Georgia woods. I imagine certain pieces of music, from waltzes like "Tales from the Vienna Woods" to the marvelous *Allegretto grazioso* from the *Symphony No. Eight* of Antonin Dvořák, and to those lines of melody I add the creatures lilting before me.

Years ago I bought a conductor's baton so I could (using scores) conduct such orchestras as the Berlin Philharmonic in my home. I have conducted the entire score of *Die Meistersinger von Nürnburg* by Richard Wagner, a four-hour opera, more than once. And I have taken my baton into the darkness to conduct the fireflies as well. What a strange and eccentric sight I must be! And yet I take such comfort from standing before these flashing creatures that I feel my heartbeat slow and my imagination soar. After a time, you start to see the fireflies fly in patterns, and the conducting affects the patterns. If I point hard to my first violins, I see fireflies fly into that section and flash madly. If I cue the tympani, the swarm heads toward the back.

I know all this is not happening, is arrant nonsense. But it seems to happen sometimes, and the jolt it gives my imagination is delicious. I see wings flapping when I have finished, applauding me.

*

Summer nights in the South are hazy, the stars usually indistinct. Sometimes the late-day clouds clear and the humidity falls and the constellations come out, but that's rare. So now it's mid-spring when the skies are still crystalline of an evening, and I am lying on my back in the side yard, in the cool dampening grass, hoping I haven't slipped into an anthill. A few small insects scurry over my legs, but they're too big to be ants so I don't worry about being stung.

Night has come. The stars overhead are brilliant and sharp. (With my glasses on, they are clear and sharp. Without my glasses, all I see are yellow blurs.) I have spotted several constellations, and I have also seen the lightning bugs begin to come out of the woods. At first there are only a few blinks, tentatively signals for mates, but within five minutes the air is spiralling with soft lights.

I have a reason for lying on the ground. I want to watch the fireflies and the stars at the same time. I often did this as a boy in the pastures out behind our house, where the sky was huge and the idea of eternity weighed on me from Sunday School and introductory science books. Since the woods crowd our house, my line of sight to the stars is limited, but it's good enough. For a moment I don't imagine music, then I'm replaying the entire *Veni Creator Spiritus* from Gustav Mahler's *Symphony No. Eight*, a work I know as well as my own blood. Suddenly there are hundreds of lightning bugs competing with billions of stars, and the lights are dazzling,

Now here's a place I'd like to have a scientist bring chaos theory to bear! Perhaps one already has, because I imagine there might be a rhythm, if not a plan, to the flight patterns. I look for recurrences, but my eye-brain coordination fails me. No matter. I let myself go in the pure delight of the moment, lie still as long as I can until it's no longer possible. I raise my arms, and the world crowds me.

But where are they before they come out flashing? It turns out that the firefly larvae overwinter in moist chambers in the forest soil where they pupate. I have never seen these secret chambers, but so much on Wildcat Ridge is secret that I am not surprised. If there is a division in the natural world between what is seen and what is unseen at any given time from any given place, then "unseen" wins every time. The visible is vast and magnificent, but it can't hold a candle to what we cannot see.

*

I lie in the grass for a very long time. Linda comes on the porch and asks me what I'm doing there, and I tell her I'm watching the lightning bugs against the background of stars.

"Mmmmmm. I need to talk with you about who's going to pick Megan up tomorrow," she says in her deep alto voice.

"Can it wait? I'm just starting to figure this out. They're spelling out a secret message meant only for me."

"Poor Megan."

"Pardon me?"

"Her father's lost his mind." I hear the front door shut and know that soon I'll have to return to the world from which I vanish sometimes.

I stand and conduct without my baton, like Leonard Bernstein. This time it's not Mahler or Dvořák, but, weirdly, the *Jamaican Rhumba* by Arthur Benjamin. And look! The lightning bugs are starting to line up and dance in a great swaying conga line! How have I done this?

I dance along with them in the grass, in the darkness, and we make our way from one shadow to the next. They clearly do not confuse me with a potential mate, but perhaps I am their Pied Piper, leading them to something holy. No. It's the other way around, I realize, as I leave them and head back inside.

Epiphany

Dr. Thomas Windall is in his early fifties, quiet and efficient. His office is large, divided into a desk area and a place where he talks with patients. I wonder what I am doing here, but I know. We chat for a moment before he cuts to the chase. "So, what's going on with you?" he asks.

Instead of telling him directly about the depths of my anxiety and depression, I describe my family history and surgery at some length, ending with the odd supposition that I inherited the curse of an early death.

"And then you found out about the heart problem?"

"Yes."

He is quiet for a moment, gathering clinical approaches. I see nothing in his eyes that seems like compassion. Mostly, he seems lost in calculation and strategies, his fingers tented just beneath his chin.

"Okay," he says finally. "Are you going to die?"

The question is shocking, so out of context that I feel a sudden anger. His demeanor is blank, except for what I read as a minor petulance. He purses his lips and looks at me directly, waiting for me to answer.

"Not now," I say hesitantly. "At least that's what they say." I am trembling with anger, and I wonder if he has laid this provocation like a military trap, to see how I will react under subtle pressure.

"And you believe them?"

"Yeah." I say it with mild sarcasm, but he's looking down at his fingers.

"Okay," he says. "So you're not going to die right away."

"No."

"Then let's talk about some things."

He leads me through a series of questions that I answer with single words wherever possible, and I watch as he shifts from one post to another. I try hard to shed my irritation and spill my guts, but I am wary and on red alert for various needlings and false trails. After a time the questioning narrows, and I feel myself relaxing back toward depression from anxiety, and there is no rest in either place. The session drones on and on, and the comfort of this room oppresses me. I want to run into the street like Kevin McCarthy in *Invasion of the Body Snatchers* and warn everyone to guard their thoughts so they won't end up like me.

I offer details, and Dr. Windall fills in holes, but neither of us offers insights. He isn't scribbling on a pad, so I wonder if we are being recorded, but he never says, and I never bring it up. I have never visited a psychiatrist before, so I hardly know how to act. I only have movies for reference.

Dr. Windall finally leans back and tents his fingers again and drums them against each other. My heart ticks for what seems like a very long time. "Would it surprise you to know you are suffering from clinical depression?" he asks.

"Yes."

"Well, you are, you know. You are dealing with a great deal here."

"And not doing it very well."

"Not as bad as you might think," he says, and for the first time I sense an edge of kindness in his voice, perhaps even sympathy. The fault of perception has no doubt been mine. "But we have a new class of drugs now that can help." He tells me about them. (I will not disclose the family of drugs or the specific trade name here because I have no desire to advertise for the pharmaceutical industry and because results vary from individual to individual.)

"So I need to be on this?" I ask.

"We do need to try it," he says. "I think you're an ideal candidate. Often, it's just a matter of brain chemistry." He gets up and walks to a cabinet and opens it to a large assortment of samples, brings me a few packs, and then writes me a prescription. He says these could make a huge difference in my state of mind.

"I'll give it a try," I say, and in a slight fog I'm out the door and into my truck.

*

My strength is returning. On nice days I walk up our long unpaved driveway through the woods to the dirt road and inhale spring, think of new projects. But I cannot write a word, cannot even climb the steps to my library and study for the first two weeks.

The first day after I begin the new medicine, I sink into mental confusion and the shakes. I don't know what I'm doing, feel heavy and out of focus. The next morning it's worse, and all day (I'm by myself now) I sit and hold on to the arms of the sofa and spin through living room galaxies, moaning but grimly determined not to stop the medicine. I feel as bad as I ever have in my life.

The second day, I am clearly sinking into despair. My hands tremble. My head seems stuffed with cotton wadding, and ghosts, heavy and familiar, crowd me as I stumble through the day. From time to time I go to bed and hold the edges of the mattress. Job-like, I cry out, asking what I have done to deserve all this, but answers don't come. A mockingbird sings his glorious bel-canto aria, but the song is not for me. I cannot sleep, so I rise and go to the bathroom and look at my face in the mirror.

"I am mad," I whisper to the reflection.

This is not adolescent drama, not some Dostoyevskian pantomime; I am making a simple statement of fact. This is my place now in the scheme of natural process, to be a howling madman, head filled with demon sounds. I walk through the woods for hope, stumble and fall. The greening canopy spins over me. I hold my head with both hands and groan. A bee droning sounds like an old warplane or a dental drill. A gentle wind burns me like a torch.

What do the creatures of Wildcat Ridge think of me? Am I special at all, or merely a large mammal dying in the late morning light? Ants and beetles would swarm me. My flesh (none too solid as it is) would melt. They would carry me down to clean, white bone, using me as they would a deer or a dog.

Is this what we come to? From an Olympian like Michelangelo to a modest pretender like me, we think we can shake off death as a dog shakes off water. But choose your metaphor: Death is our shadow and companion, our scourge, our haven. We owe God a death.

*

I get up and thrash my way from the forest into the yard. The oaks are leafing, though the elm by the front door is still bare. My head is so heavy it could fall off any moment and roll down the hill. Inside, I sit and put my hands in my lap and watch the clock hands do their work. When Linda asks how I am doing with the medicine, I lie reasonably well, tell her that I don't feel better yet. I want to reveal the slope on which I stand, but I am afraid, and she already has enough problems dealing with our children.

*

On the third day, the despair lifts somewhat, but I am still edgy and even a little paranoid. I have not stopped the medicine, will not stop until it kills me or I get well. During the morning I feel a reckless urge to go driving, to see something distracting, and so I dress slowly, careful not to overstretch the wires that still hold my breastbone together. I am not really supposed to be driving yet, but my need for flight is paramount. Ingrained. Perhaps I am migrating.

For the first time since my surgery, I drive through the countryside and look at the new face of spring. It is March. Nights can remain cold here, but the days are deliciously warm. I look at this land and think of my ancestors, breaking up the soil with mule teams, stoic wives cooking before dawn. They felt the rhythm of farm life, the cycle of birth and death, loved God, climbed the ladder of hope toward Heaven. Unexpectedly, I am driving toward town, and I simply give the truck its head, as one might a horse. Where am I going? What will become of me? I feel almost all right now, and I am afraid to look far into the pathology of it.

I drive through Watkinsville, up toward Athens, and I realize that what I miss is not the citizenry of the forest, but human contact; I crave my own kind. At stoplights I see them in their most ordinary guises. Students from the university hustle toward bus stops. A woman puts on lipstick before the light changes. An old man walks on the Milledge Avenue sidewalk, elbows out, long white beard lifted slightly by wind in the sharp sunlight. I get to a stoplight, and I am staring at the leaves on a water oak and a thought forms itself, rises in me from somewhere very deep, still, and dark: *It sure is a beautiful day.*

Suddenly, in a light that is stunningly unexpected, the feeling hits me, the same lifting and awakening I had when I was eight years old. Happiness fills me. I am dry-eyed and clear-eyed. Time slows into a sweet crawl.

"Oh *please*," I beg, not wanting the feeling to fail me, but it cannot, and I know it.

I am aware instantly that this is an altering of brain chemistry from the medicine, but I don't care. I feel like myself, like me, for the first time in months, maybe years. The world is a hymn. I drive slowly forward, but I am dazzled by the unseen love and the promise of new days, and I do not come even close to tears. And the day is so lovely! The leaves move so gently in the wind!

I am falling in love with the possibility of life.

*

I drive to a nearby park, get out, and walk around the pond. I take my ticking heart on a slow journey, muttering *thank you, thank you* over and over. The morning is glorious, and I am part of its enduring light. I think of my family and imagine future scenes. I consider a new novel, perhaps a cycle of poems. I want to see the Rocky Mountains.

Home is a long drive, and I go inside and put on Beethoven's *Symphony No. Seven*, which has one of the most joyous finales I know. I don't want to believe I am healing, but I am.

*

Mostly, I think of Linda, off teaching her eighth graders, and I cannot wait to tell her my secret, to reveal that I am going to live.

Country

Those city-born and -bred might find amusement in my fascination with the kingdoms of country. And I do not claim my closeness to natural process makes me a wiser man or more fit for survival. But, to me, suburbs and city streets are not fit context for a full life. I have found I cannot flourish with too much noise or human contact, that I am embraced most passionately by the silence of the countryside. This is a world chosen for me by generations of men and women who broke the soil, felt close to the woods and the fields.

Moving to town has become encrusted with myth among southerners because for many it meant escape from poverty and ignorance into fellowship and acceptance by humankind. My own father's family moved to town three generations ago, turning their backs on the knuckle-cracking work of farming. Leisure time came late to these men and women, but stories most certainly did not. And they must have retained that love of country in music or stories, must have dreamed themselves back into the furrows and jangling mule harnesses, to the smell of cooking blackberries and the lovely discord of hymns from the open windows of small churches in summer.

My country was not brought to me on memory or tradition. I was raised on a country road in the 1950s, borne by an insular world that no longer exists. When I was seven years old, I would take off in the morning for the woods and stay all day, and my mother never worried for my safety one moment. We boys thrilled to the re-creation of cowboy movies and combat newsreels. We built our own baseball diamond in the cow pasture, with croaker-sack bases and an outfield as far as a dream.

I learned to build a campfire, to sleep among the night noises, to tie a solid knot, I discovered I took no pleasure in the hunt, though fishing brought me to the surface of some enduring waterway to the past. We picked up potsherds and arrowheads; they bound us to those who lived here long before and who are now largely forgotten, even in our schools. I learned birds and beasts and tracks.

My parents also led me gently to art in that country, to Wordsworth and Keats and e.e. cummings, to Bach and Beethoven and hymnody. I still remember being stunned at age nine by Dali's *Persistence of Memory*, reproduced in a set of encyclopedias we owned. I never felt any dichotomy between country and the arts. I never believed that a city could fill the gaps of my life.

*

And so we came to Wildcat Ridge. Until the day I first saw the house and land, I did not know how much I had lost by living in town. All my life I have been heading for the country, not to re-create a happy childhood, but to grant myself the gift of hawks, the geography of flowing water.

I have come into that presence with singing. Having spent many years among scientists, I have also come into it with a hunger for telling details, for the process that turns so grandly in the cycles of an ecosystem. I have learned my place well enough. On good days, I still believe man may be the measure of all things, and I stand speechless before the works of the mighty. On other days, I accept with fine spirits our late arrival as a species, our lumbering stupidities, our brassy presumption. I do not love nature in order to hate humanity. I make connections to fulfill the prophecies of time and species. Crown me the village idiot for conducting an orchestra of fireflies. I will not mind.

*

Who claims the forest? It claims itself.

*

I am an ecologist without portfolio. I am merely an interested amateur, but I honor the scientists who spend their lives as specialists, whether of a worm or a molecule. They are links, and we need their focus to understand what this floral and faunal chain finally binds.

We unschooled lovers of nature often misunderstand, misdiagnose. We slip in taxonomy, confuse one constellation with another. We misidentify a fleabane, understand little of ants or bats. We *are* sometimes the source for knowledge, sometimes accidentally. Perhaps, though, we may be a model for ardor, may bring the seasoning of exuberance and joy that professionals often lose along the way.

*

No skyscraper is as lovely or complex as a passionflower. No sonata is as beautifully layered as a hornet's nest.

I have come to these conclusions twice in my life, both times in the heart of the country. If I am nostalgic toward my childhood, I feel unsentimental toward nature. I hear no Bambi or Thumper. Still, I see a raveling cloak of gorgeous light, stories of moss and stone and wind. I am consumed by the fables of insects.

In a time I was dying, Wildcat Ridge held me up above the canopy of oak and poplar and sweet gum and pine. It also took my roots into the richer soil and held them until the whisper of decay was gone. I would not die, not yet. I come from this burrow into the sanctity of green.

Final Things

I sit in a beach house on Jekyll Island as I write these last words in the summer of 1997. The sun has not yet risen from the green waters of the Atlantic, but light comes strong from the east. A shrimp boat leans against its nets, slowly struggling down the coast.

Three years and more have passed since I found my heart was failing. Six years on Wildcat Ridge. Some days, distance is the only cure, but today we are heading home after a week here watching the tides rise and fall. We have watched birds arrive on the deck for Linda's inevitable handouts. A band of feral cats has adopted us, and she and Megan have been feeding them Purina Cat Chow and leftover macaroni.

My wife is an ardent shell collector, and she has found bags of miniature spires, or whelks and lady-slippers and scallop shells. At a beach on the south end of the island, we discovered dozens of shells filled with their tenants: small, secretive crabs. We took none of them, nor did we take the living sand dollars. We interfere with natural process enough already. We have exulted in wave and dune, but I am ready for the red dust of a north Georgia summer. I want to see the land where I learned to heal.

*

Brandon is now nineteen, will be a sophomore in college this fall. Megan is nearing six and will enter public kindergarten. I have watched them grow with a delight I cannot express.

Megan earlier in the week lay against me on the sofa as we watched television. "I can hear your ticky heart," she said. Then, "Why did they give you a ticky heart?"

"My old one was broken," I said, hugging my brown-eyed darling closer to me. "So they fixed me."

"Okay."

We had no need for other words. This is not merely modern medicine to me. It is miraculous.

*

I took the drug for my depression for less than a year, then slowly weaned myself off it. The depression finally faded into my own history, though dark days still come and go as they do for anyone else. But I have worked hard and loved those dear to me. I have settled a few issues with God.

All my life, shadows have pursued me, whispered of legendary early deaths, of Keats and Shelley and Uncle Sambo and my Grandfather Williams. I no longer look over my shoulders, though.

The meaning of this life may come to me someday in a moment of grace or brilliant illumination, but I doubt it. And I do not mind that notable absence. I had rather know the etymology of birdcalls, the language of deer. I will read the Braille of shadows. I will attach the music of nineteenth-century Europe to a herd of fireflies, wave my baton to give myself order. I will invent fanciful theories, reattach the stars into new constellations.

My body is a new territory as well. Because of the Coumadin—my line to this life—I bruise very easily, and some days I resemble an ancient map, with the shapes of countries or continents on body or legs.

I must take good care of this animal that carries me.

*

I don't seek homilies from the red-tailed hawk or lessons from bats on Wildcat Ridge. I do believe that each plant or animal is a puzzle-part in the picture of meaning. And that picture is not a two-dimensional, tabletop image but a ziggurat with an exoskeleton and a maze of internal rooms.

Still, I come to this land and its quiet creek for comfort, and I use it as evidence of order and therefore of God. In my first published novel, *The Heart of a Distant Forest*, I wrote, "A man's religion is nobody else's damn business." To me, religion is a place that may only be found with a lifetime of searching, and even then it is elusive. I would no more tell a man which faith to follow than I would tell him what shirt to wear. But I don't hold with those who think the journey can be made only with the precise map of ancient thought. We must seek our makers.

I lay upon you lightly the idea that nature is one marker on your trip. It is the context in which we flourish or fail as animals. It is a compass, not toward Moral True North but toward process and place.

A man whose heart fails him in mid-life is no more uncommon than a raccoon that eats sea turtle eggs, licking up the sweet liquid that—given time—might have been another thing entirely. We change, we live or die, we move on.

We are all crossing Wildcat Ridge.

*

Megan plays in the waves near dusk. Few people are out here on the vanishing lip of sand as the tide rises. The sea is green near shore, changing to slate gray farther out.

Jekyll is a barrier island, filled with live oaks, pines, and red cedars. We have rented a house on the beach for a week with Linda's parents, Fred and Marie Rowley, and they are wonderful company. Now, Megan screams with each breaking wave, falling flat in the churn of small shells and foam. I stand not far away, looking at the rising half-moon and the expansive cirrus clouds that drift in their ice lace miles above us. Before I know it, Megan is standing next to me. "Are those God's wings?" she asks, pointing to the clouds. I smile at the idea but don't laugh.

"I don't know," I say. "I don't think so. I think they're just clouds. Where do you think God lives?"

"Far away up there," she says, "FAR, FAR!" She raises her arms high to indicate magnitude.

"Might be," I say. "I kind of think God's a place inside us."

"*Huh*," she says, and she's off into the waves, falling, coming up like a cherub version of Botticelli's shell maiden.

*

Each day, each morning I roll from bed, is a gift. Yesterday I went alone to the beach, and it was high tide and no one was visible, north or south. I watched the waves for a long time and thought of how quickly we pass from this world, and I felt no sadness from it. I thought of my generations gone and perhaps to come, and I considered the seabirds, the churning of crab and calcareous shell. I knew my ignorance was vast, and I did not mind so much. I will never cure cancer or heart disease, and I do not know if I will ever truly relieve another's burden. I only know that I have seen a red-tailed hawk in flight, have watched the creek dunes form themselves in rising and falling splendor like the kingdoms of Egypt.

And I understand finally that a life well lived is an act of praise. If I endure among the living, it will be in the words of my children and the sound of a freshening wind in the treetops on Wildcat Ridge.